BY DAVID MELTZER

POETRY

Poems (w/Donald Schenker)
(1957)
Ragas (1959)
The Clown (1960)
The Process (1965)
The Dark Continent (1967)
Round the Poem Box (1969)
Yesod (1969)
From Eden Book (1969)
Greenspeech (1970)
Luna (1970)
Knots (1971)

Bark (1973)
Tens, Selected Poems: 1961-71
(1973)
Hero/Lil (1973)
The Eyes, The Blood (1973)
Blue Rags (1974)
Harps (1975)
Six (1976)
The Art, The Veil (1981)
Arrows: Selected Poetry
1957-1992 (1994)

FICTION

The Agent (1968)
The Agency (1968)
How Many Blocks in the Pile?
(1969)
Orf (1969)
The Martyr (1969)

Lovely (1969)
Healer (1969)
Out (1969)
Glue Factory (1969)
Star (1970)

ESSAYS

We All Have Something to Say to Each Other: An Essay on
Kenneth Patchen (1962)
Bazascope Mother (On Robert Alexander) (1964)
Journal of the Birth (1967)
Isla Vista Notes (1970)
Two-Way Mirror: A Poetry Notebook (1977)

CHILDREN'S TALES

Abra (illustrated by John Brandi) (1976)

TRANSLATION

Morning Glories by Shiga Naoya (in collaboration with
Allen Say) (1976)

ANTHOLOGIES

The San Francisco Poets (1971)
Golden Gate: Interviews with Five San Francisco Poets
(1976)
The Secret Garden: Anthology of the Classical Kabbalah
(1976)
The Path of the Names: Writings by Abraham ben Samuel
Abulafia (1976)
Birth: An Anthology of Ancient Texts, Songs, Prayers, and
Stories (1981)
Death: An Anthology of Texts, Songs, Charms, Prayers, and
Stories (1984)

DAVID MELTZER
ARROWS

SELECTED POETRY 1957–1992

BLACK SPARROW PRESS ◀ SANTA ROSA ▶ 1994

LIBRARY OF CONGRESS CATALOGING-IN-PUBLICATION DATA

Meltzer, David.
  Arrows: selected poetry 1957-1992 / David Meltzer.
    p.   cm.
    ISBN 0-87685-939-2 (cloth trade) : — ISBN 0-87685-940-6 (signed cloth ed.)
  : — ISBN 0-87685-938-4 (pbk.) :
    I. Title.
  PS3563.E45A6   1994
  811'.54—dc20   94-26540
                                                                CIP

The first "book" contains poems written from 1957—my first book, *Poems*, shared with Donald Schenker's work (printed by Don and Alice on Weldon Kees' letterpress on Potrero Hill)—to 1973, *The Eyes, the Blood* published by Bob and Eileen Callahan's Mudra Press (designed and printed by Clifford Burke of Cranium Press, one of many Bay Area resources generous to poetry).

Works in the second "book" often reflect the texture and darkening *umwelt* of the 1980s and 90s; some, like *Arrows* and *Bakelite*, are more conscious reflections of (and metaphors for) the politics of the period.

I'd like to dedicate this book to the students and faculty of New College of California.

D. M.

Table of Contents

BOOK ONE

1. From *Poems* (1957)
   "There never was a sin that did not commit
         itself"   17
   Oration at the Funeral of a Chinese Youth   18
   Poem for Idell   19
   From the Untitled Epic Poem   20

2. From *Ragas* (1959)
   30th June: 59   23
   Vision   26
   Mexico   27
   2nd Raga: The Woods   30
   4th Raga: Revelation   30
   From: Night Before Morning   31
   15th Raga: For Bela Lugosi   34
   The Mechanikons   35
   6th Raga: For Bob Alexander   38

3. From *The Process* (1965)
   A Poem for My Wife   41
   "This morning"   42
   Self Portrait   42
   The Blackest Rose   43
   Youth Rite Reels   44
   A Rent Tract: For Lew Welch   46
   Chthonic Fragments: For George Herms   47
   Tishah B'ov/1952   49
   Oyez! (December 1965)   51

4. From *The Dark Continent* (1967)
   For Zap the Zen Monk (1960)   55
   For Lenny Bruce   56
   For Celine   57
   For Hank Williams   59
   For Jack Spicer   60

5. From *Round the Poem Box: Rustic & Domestic Home Movies for Stan & Jane Brakhage* (1969)
   Fanfare   63
   Election Day TV   64
   The Argument: 1   65
   The Argument: 2   65
   Sonnet: 3   66
   Nature Poem   67
   Another Argument   68
   I'm greedy. I lie. I cheat. I'm afraid of failure.
        Is it true I also steal?   69

6. From *Yesod* (1969)
   Return   73
   For Raymond Chandler   74

7. *The Eyes, the Blood* (1973)   75

BOOK TWO

1. *Arrows*
   " 'Eros' backwards 'sore' "   91
   "Postcard: pale blue synthetic"   92
   "need for a whip her mouth eats"   92
   "language invents heaven"   93
   "Arose a Rose"   93
   "who follows flows easily"   94
   "Nazi leather riding crop"   94
   "power against powerlessness"   95
   "fingernails dig into palm meat"   95
   "any body anywhere an eye cocks"   96
   "impact barrier threshold boundary"   96
   "master discourse master matrix"   97
   "stick pins in your dick on the phone"   97

2. *Bakelite*   99

3. *Monkey*   115

4. *Pardes*   121

5. *Others*
    "cops everywhere"   135
    It's Simple   135
    Night Reels   136
    Kabbalistic Tree Poem for R. Skratz   137
    For Ibn 'Arabi   138
    13 iv 90   139
    "maker of riddles and little else"   143
    "heart portioned finally shredded . . ."   144
    "how to break the slug in two"   145
    "Stamped on / Stravinsky's / birthday"   146
    "wood heart sound-board Bach Suite"   147
    Pre-   148
    "old love pain chaos . . ."   150
    "Who bends the broken branch back into
        place"   150
    "poem's progress out the door"   151
    "dark oblong blinking book mass"   152
    "no more war"   153
    "who's the jew . . ."   154
    "the poetry that starts"   156
    "old reds . . ."   157
    Commute   159
    "Now sweet when it should be sour"   160
    "Alone as the street denies touch"   160
    "the pain in paper . . ."   161

6. From *The Art / The Veil* (1981)
   The Veil
    "so sheer between what's right"   167
    "In the hole he counted heartbeats"   167
    "The veil"   168
    "It was perfect"   168
    "The veil"   169
    "The scar"   169
    "The veil"   170
    "How cold"   170
    "The piercing"   171

The Art
"Organizing these myths these trends these"   175
"Once"   175
"It's easier to say nothing"   176
"Cigarette smoke in my hair"   176
"Noisily yank a failed poem out of the
    typewriter roller."   177
"It isn't fame or failure"   177
"Dawn loon silhouette"   178
"The deception of a new typewriter ribbon"   178
"The hunt"   179
"There's a Europe he holds"   179
"All the light"   180
"Some enter and never leave"   180
"What's given up"   181
"I go through my body and out onto paper"   181
Note   182

7. *Notes*
K-K-K-A-O-S: Lecture Notes (Biodegradable Prose
    Specks)   185
Millennial   190

ARROWS:

SELECTED POETRY, 1957-1992

— BOOK ONE —

1.

From *Poems* (1957)

◆

There never was a sin that did not commit itself
after it was over
and some damn poet saying no to yes
held a looking glass to naked bodies
yelling see yourselves
to those naked bodies
secretly being themselves

ORATION AT THE FUNERAL OF A CHINESE YOUTH

Block-puzzle
enigma of splinters
stand back before you open up
the bundled corpse of a child

his dying smile of incense
smells of rot
and slicked-back sideburns form
twin islands on his skull

Asian mismatch made the maze
and came through poker-faced

nowhere is brighter than the end
nothing is more promising

POEM FOR IDELL

anotherwords
depending on the shape and motion of words
linked together, a wreath
tight to the tearing of time

anotherwords
to place experience on the page of death
filed in a reaching sequence
unfolding like a stair

anotherwords
to teach with words unspeakable meanings
leading away and into yourself

to violate churches
piss on their silks and sticks of pain
to violate and make holy

anotherwords
afterwards
in darkness a way of making your light
upon living shadows

a way to confuse conclusion
refusing to end it
stating again and again
until it limps to whisper
ghost directions everywhere

FROM THE UNTITLED EPIC POEM

Somewhere, waiting to be found; a bar-mitzvah of hopeless-
ness in the Waldorf Cafeteria, hungering for a chance to
detonate New York, return the Masses to themselves; hunger-
ing, waiting to be found, rejoicing in Joyce because he con-
fused, little magazines because they refused, rejecting the
scholar who seemed too safe, all-knowing; sitting in the Wal-
dorf Cafeteria wondering where Bohemia was, in some back
alley of the Village waiting to be stumbled into.

Youngest radical to join the back lines, waiting for a
chance to step out of line and proclaim an action that never
happened; to throw a bomb into the marble echo of a Bank,
or tie TNT to the Brooklyn Bridge at rush hour, to topple the
statue of George Washington in Wall Street; start a chain-
reaction of burning dresses in the Garment Center; to free the
enslaved; enslave the enslavers; to do anything, but to do
something final.

Folk-singing prophets in mid-afternoon: sandal squeaking
ventriloquists of the proletariat; Zionist zombies sipping es-
presso; Itkin, the impossible, on the steps of a Catholic Church,
confused by Eliot, wishing he wasn't queer; the lisp and laugh
of fairies snipping perfume through the streets; sequin bitch-
ery, the tough humor of survivors; night of blackened days,
Benzedrine blues, and early morning flowers on the street,
walking home and stepping on scattered petals.

Black uniforms; danced in the Waldorf, turned-on in the
Automat, threw ourselves in front of the A train; we were liv-
ing visions of weekly suicides, crawling into hangouts with
dripping bandages.

Somewhere, waiting to be found, we fooled the fakirs, were
kings of the underworld; maggots in some armpit; no loving,
only the desire for love, and the waiting.

Genesis one, the beginning; we would go away, discover
Zen, Spiritualism, the positive, the negative, whisper of Sartre
and the Paris Existentialism. I followed, failed to find, and no
one celebrated my bar-mitzvah in the Waldorf Cafeteria, not
even myself.

2.

From *Ragas* (1959)

In Memory of Frederick Roscoe

30TH JUNE: 59

Dear Wally,

My family tree rots with dead & shrunken fruit. Filled with things that chew, devour actual facts. Dead fruit, dried-up fruit, dropping to the dusty ground. My family tree: a crooked shadow, a wooden hand, arthritic.

My grandfather's reptile touch, my grandmother's bloated knuckles; my father scratching scabs in swirls around his greyhaired belly; my mother weeping on the kitchen floor, casting away the black butcher knife.

Dry roots suck into dry ground. The earth's a powder, held uneasily by dust, rocks, ghosts. — Is there any hope? Hope in my crosseyed vision of Nirvana? — No. I'm a nest of barbed-wire, no leaf or flower comforts, I hear death work inside the cracking branch.

No hope in making, assembling, binding together ornate bibles of history. The clues are everywhere outside the printed word, inside the sleeping poet; on the streets, beneath the sea; in levels, stratum, the pages of a desert; an aura around the dead buried within our memories.

— * —

Reconsider the wind moving flags, an invisible snake shuttling through the grass.

Reconsider poems taken up by the wind, carried into the sky as clouds. Shadows bend backwards disappearing.

A poem challenges nothing. Bends in the wind. Seed carrying insects bomb quiet gardens with golden missiles. A poem from each nailhole. Tied by roots and weeds to bind myth together.

Birds connect the heavens. Clouds filter shadows into rainbow halos circling the rolling earth, but the eye sees outside. Stars and poets chasing the earth to its ends.

To howl with the coyote is to howl the true song throughout desert nights. Infinity. Is that what the ancient song sings? A cowboy on his broken-backed mare.

To relent song. Be silent. Approach peace pure of all kinds of shit. Or carry the wheelbarrow to it.

— * —

It comes to nothing outside your self. Nobody knows what the machine really said. Everyone listens to the mechanikons work gears and gimmick inside plastic hearts; tongues multiply a restricted message.

Loud and ignorant, I sit in my monkey box, drawing murals using snot from my runny nose.

The fur-trapper who cut out his own appendix, holding a mirror in one hand, hacking at the pain with the other. THE PAIN MUST BE REMEDIED! And off he goes to work. No doctor, phone, or Red Cross bible. Just the immediate need to
break wind into
flowers, grab what's visible, shape it. Isn't that enough?

— * —

the quartergrain spreads inside slowly, seeps & sops through those hunks of meat & spacious flesh weave, & the mind's arc widens to include each demented animal, each distorted figurine, each word, each measure, each rock, each zero

Mandarin O Mandarin! No one's wiser than zero. Only the machine tabulating flesh, chewing it up, fucking, squashing, healing the wound before it opens! What a gyp, what a lousy gyp! Screwed out of my own pain watching TV.

— * —

Yearn: brooks & words of clearest water

—Did he eat up the other end?
—He was the other end, he ate himself up all ways.
All together. He ate himself up to nothing. He's now in the process of becoming holy for the others.
Space & air. The words
humming there. A beard growing from a tree. When the branch

24

cracks, the nest falls, turns to dust, grows backasswards into the soil, back to the core. So what? Blind moles will take pods deeper into the possible blackness. Termites in each eye: thumb levers to light.

Love,
David

VISION

The heart sees what the mind sees what the eyes see
differently

MEXICO

O nerve! open, WIDE, sore, RAW
aching with moon   Maze
     MAYA(n)   stoned eyes
     of stone God, fat force of Art
     squashing me down   Mouth
     of Jaguar
Ornamented hide of the Great Snake

Poets (ghosts) in the jungle.
Faces pasted on with leaves from great iguana
banana, cocoa-nut trees.   Ghosts
with the hot afternoon. Vapors
steam out of dry land near the river
(constant water: birds, sounds of freak things
growing wings, unclassified)   Mud of the river
frothing like horseshit.   Flies,
insects   A humming curtain
Vultures—gods—float in a grey sky
mean yellow eyes

     NERVE?
Doc Oachilix inserts the blade quickly.
Gangrene opens its comicbook smile.
Blood. Chewing a black pebble,
sharpening my teeth. He
peels away my arm and leg flesh.
—See? Now watch:

The Doc sprinkles sun-dried seeds into shining raw
muscles
—mouths of gaping sea animals, strange & misplaced.
—See? Now watch, he says in Spanish/English
Both.   All language sickens in the fever spot.
A circle burning through my brain

       WITCHES   !   FLOWERS
       a song in each powdery root
       grows in the valleys of my wounds.

My legs move, grabbed by petals
rubber wings, wings of a mad lunar bird
—See?

with scalpel, lancet
Dr Oachilix

(Todos the nurse is there—hands Doc the needle)

Old Tijuana whore, go shave your head!
breathes cavities, American perfumes

Doc drills into my cornea

SUN
      MOON
            DREAM   .   River

Stone God fat by chisel
fat by marking, the artist hand
forcing Art into its skull

Sun
Vulture
Yellow mean eyes

—See. You hear? Yes, listen
bleed, corrupt, devour, rot.
Go mad. Be buried alive,
livid with flowers growing cancer.

NURSE!

but they're busy on the floor—
she's ripping off his face—
he's sucking her orange teat
babbling Mexican/English
language of the stoned God.

Understood.
Stone God Flat Top laughs, heaves up
great stone boulders of laughter.
Death and no manuscript.
No note, relic, no
anthropo-archeao-logical hint
left behind.
Only my teeth, my bones
the fish'll spit out.

—See?

2ND RAGA: THE WOODS

It's morning. I awaken
fart, reach for last night's joint
cradled in the ashtray & turn on.
                 The sun through trees
surround the house on Vashon Island.
                          Exhaling, I think
today I'll go to the wild patch & pick a bowl
full of strawberries for breakfast

4TH RAGA: REVELATION

It comes to this: a teacup
filled with hot green tea.
Basho beside me with poised *ohashi*
waiting for Reiko to bring out
the *nikku nabe,* the *sake,* some Kirin Beer.

The haiku come later
after dinner & a Havatampa cigar.

FROM: NIGHT BEFORE MORNING

Other instruments accompany a slow morning:
lute, tine hand-bells, Jew's harp, trump, bandora
kithara

(Solomon played it dipping his feet in a green constant
        brook)

ORPHEUS' VERY OWN LYRE!   LOOK
    BIRD'S EYE POEM SEE-ALL HIGH!

            A bundle of rags, a caravan
animals, singers, gilt & gold ash, hawk & eagle
feathers drop on dusty roads. A wooden wheeled circus
moves along to drums of dead sound mute with steady
bhm. bhm. bhm.
bells, recorders, wood whistles, mellow bird song
Riu, riu. chiu/Pari forma   (Not
                the kid with rickets in looted Ike jacket
                stands, one foot stiff, upon rubble of a great
                fallen Neapolitan cathedral singing
                Shoo Fly Pie & Apple Pan Dowdy
                for a can of powdered eggs)
tambourines, triangle, treble viol

Brooding in a cage hooked
above Master's trunk
a one-legged parrot
whose rancid wings
sulk into passive folds.
Tongue widens inside its old chipped beak.

A lice-fevered Bear

                —They put these big leather boots on his big
                stinky feet. Tear his claws out—even his
                dumb teeth are fake.   DANCE!
Not for a parade, the music

(Down Columbus Avenue, no horses
instead: Simonized Cadillac convertibles draped in paper
       flowers
painted plaster Madonnas, banners hanging from door
       handles

            The Majorette is 12.
            Her kneecaps greased with salt & dirt.
            Sun illuminates glaring silk, brightly
            illustrates gold & thin black hairs
            on her legs, her arms

followed by the North beach Junior High School R. O. T. C.
       Brass
Auxiliary Band
paratroopers marching through Roma
tubas, trumpets, trombones, drums, coronets
followed by

the St Francis Parochial Girls School Percussion Band
yellow & green silk braid holding up their drums
snare, bass, kettle, cymbals, triangle, cowbells)

Not for a parade, the music
but for the dance!
Jubilate Deo omnis terra!

Puncta . puncta . bhm. bhm. bhm.

            (passing the Dunkit Donut Shop
where teenage tigers in DAs linger, drink coffee, smoke
look out the window to see highschool girls waggle by
on the way to Big Boy Supermarket. The jukebox)

Regular measure, dance beat, *estampie*
echoes in the hall of fiddles, trumpets
shawm & viol. Tumblers & acrobats! Jugglers
toss porcelain balls into vaulted air.
Bean a demon! (Rock a baby rock a baby
rock a baby bye

32

Motorcycle S.F.P.D. pulls against the curb.
Black uniform, white crash helmet
high noons into Dunkit) *Salterello*

peasants wild with wine dance off to bed or
secret cove behind lemon trees. The Bear
pukes   —Everytime, everytime
someone slips him a sip of homebrew
& the dumb beast starts in

Bazza Danza: formal peace glide and flow
for whoever's left.
Wagons shake with lovers, bushes crackle.
Who's left, Traditionalists
dance the slow dance right as if the Queen
were spying through a square lens scope,
seawaves & leaping dolphins etched in gold.

Bhm. *Puncta.* BHM!
            Caravan breaks camp, starts
            moving through night.
            Tinderboxes clack.
            Here

hawk wingtip tickling my cheek
reels of astrology weave warm stars along the road
the trees hide everything else from the birds

15TH RAGA: FOR BELA LUGOSI

Sir, when you say
Transylvania or wolfbane or
I am Count Dracula,
your eyes widen &, for the moment,
become pure white marble.

No wonder you were a junkie.
It's in the smile. Your way of drifting
into Victorian bedrooms
holding up your cape like skirts,
then covering her face
as you bent over to kiss & sup.

It is no wonder & it was
in good taste too.

THE MECHANIKONS

HOW FAR DOWN? Deep, the old litho-plate
eaten by gold acids, underground editions of
*La Bas, Le Fleurs Du Mal, L'Illuminations,
Un Saison en Enfer,* or the carbolic
spirit of the diabolical in a red silk
lounging jacket, open, showing a white chest,
a minimum of hair: designs
against the white

      roues of basement clubs
      torture racks & whips
      wall hooks to hang meat upon
      candles in blackened bronze claws
      A vat dripping absinthe
      Tribal meeting of rats
      Spiderwebs Theremin Opium
      smoke ghosts hovering, nuzzling
      grainy ceilings   Satan
      a gargoyle growing through the wall

Yes, decay is action. His trenchmouth
sours the tongue, the Poet
watches the rose die—for days & nights—smokes tin after
tin of scented cigarettes
Yellow smoke drifts filter the rot of the rose
—of course: the full moon

of Oz, yellow, orange, bespectacled, hides
behind dusty curtains holding an Oriental
jade-handled knife, waiting

        — * —

The Vampyr—his blackbird soul—suspended,
a Rorschach shadow on her pale cheek. Hawk
combats sky, the mountain—iron wings,
leather smile—& finds a cave & a coffin
to brood upon til morning.   —FEED ME

blood, the final connection, the purest energy
constant within your glass flesh—Dracula
rolls up his velvet sleeve to suck on scabs,
kiss drab red mouths. Burning
wash of rainbow-stains beneath above the spoon
Sulphur   A green bug tracks through the sugar
A glass of water, dust net surface   Photograph:
death-mask of Proust, pipe from a Tibetan cave,
triptych of three found faces, no mirrors, pictures,
paintings, scrolls, & a teakwood drawer
stuffed with hand-painted antique slides &
classic pornography. Spherical music
from a machine, Gregorian monks,
their hemp skirts slide through fall leaves

                    — * —

Then to sleep, the lover with Poe's eyes, anointed
carried thru the cobblestoned city
on the faceless shoulders of women
smelling of olives, all with hairy mouths
who spread out on stuffed settees for their lizard lover
the eyes of Poe, Rimbaud's mouth against their hips
tongues of blackness, songs of secrets,
flesh stretched to oblivion

A thousand alleyways with walk-down doorways
signs of stars in formation, signs of hands
Sol on a plank over the window
REMOVED)   To sleep.   The snakes
nest in stained sheets. The Lover
lust turns fat around his rims, upon his jaws,
heavy on his harp tongue-tip
fattened penis, null & grey as the hair.
Decay is action. Paper flowers
stale bread; Dante's hand.
White hair, roots rest in sand—inertia
will pull the head off onto the pile of clothes

— * —

Gracefully, the powered hammer drives
The Flash
O vein receive this waterfall galloping through me
twenty tons of twenty horses galloping through

Flash of it
Fist of the Sphinx
Her paw with grace drives shut the Crypt

and with steam shovel
buries the sleeping traveler alive.
Sand in his mouth, he dare not
protest

6TH RAGA: FOR BOB ALEXANDER

Cigarette gone, you walked over
to the stain where the sea last hit
the shore and, with your fingers,
drew the outline of a woman.
Her breasts, a poke inside each center
for her nipples; her cunt,
a simple v, and her hair
a spray of seaweed found nearby.

Jumping back, the sea rushing in,
you yelled something I didn't hear.
We turned our backs to the Pacific,
back up to Ocean Front Avenue.
Charlie was waiting with his camera.
Altoon arrived with a six-pack of
good old Lucky Lager beer.

3.

From *The Process* (1965)

For Robert and Dorothy Hawley

A POEM FOR MY WIFE

I'm in my room writing
speaking in myself & I hear you
move down the hallway to water your plants

I write truth on the page
striking the word over & over
yet worry you'll pour too much water on the plants
& the water will overflow onto the books
ruining them

If I can't speak out of myself
how can I tell you
I don't care about the plants?
how can I tell you
I don't care if the books get wet?

We've been together over seven years
& only now do I begin
clearing my throat to speak to you.

♦

This morning

waking to quiet the kids
last night's seed
a trail of light down your thighs.

SELF PORTRAIT

on the window
facing a wall of wood slats

aww the hell with it!
recognize the limit

2, 3 feet ahead of me: me
my face on the glass
looking up

THE BLACKEST ROSE

I'm afraid of the flowers, she said
  they move so quietly.

Vines on the bedtable
  Roses on the dresser
Awaken at night as my breath awaits love

The flowers turn
  (Breathing as they move)
Towards me, in the dark
  Large shadows

I'm afraid of the breath the flowers take,
  she said
New moon tonight, I watch without sleep
  So quietly do they move upon me

YOUTH RITE REELS

Farewell, my friends, my path inclines to this side of the moun-
tain, yours to that. For a long time you have appeared further
and further off to me. I see that you will at length disappear
altogether.

—Thoreau: *Journals*

1.

Home's grip chokes me dizzy
I pound walls to leave this room.

Oak dresser mirror watches an open window.

Road going into a hill
& beyond it,

the radium of cities.

2.

In the bus, Greyhound Deluxe,
one bathroom for all, small
lights overhead like flashlights.
I can't read my book. Passing
black forms, small towns, city neon.
Passing around a cheap fifth of vodka.
Discharged today, two soldiers try
to get everyone drunk. In the dark
someone starts to sing O Susannah.
I go to sleep in Ohio, wake up in Omaha.
There's snow all around us
in piles ten feet high.

3.

Factory smoke & jet trails
mark the blue with ghosts. Moving
towards the city, the car

goes too fast. Its driver
beeps the horn twice. No reason.
This is the way to drive. Rock and roll
on the radio, wind thru the window,
cigarette sparks.

Wheels turn, I feel them, on a bump,
springs shake, leaving the sun behind.
Thick clouds form, black
rims slam against sun shafts,
passing by the Edge Motel
(in construction) a broken
water line pissing up into
the coming storm.

4.

I sing to them, the old men, their faces
worn as mesas, mouths
thin as razor slices, manage
can after can of Pearl Beer.
10 gallons half-mast, tiny
Roy Roger eyes gleam in shadow.
They await my flute solo.
Mud in boot, I dance from their bullets.
Shaman, it ain't fair,
turn me into a jackrabbit. I cry,
the sky so beautifully blue, with two
torn clouds hanging, ready to fall.

A RENT TRACT: FOR LEW WELCH

At the first of the month I go to the Rental Agency. —Listen, I tell her, —I can't pay this month's rent because I quit my job at the bookstore because I have a great work I'm working on that demands a tremendous amount of all of my time. My job was a rock in my heart, a black cloud in my head, and I'm a poet, I need solitude, solo time to wander, study, loaf, drink, think, read, love my wife, learn about my kids, and work every day and every night on my great work. It's like this, I gave this month's rent to my wife for food, diapers, and wine. Why don't you forget about it until my great work is done?

—Sure, she said, writing a check for $229, the exact amount needed to tide us thru a month. —& come back at the first of next month for your next check, she said & turned back to her ledger.

CHTHONIC FRAGMENTS: FOR GEORGE HERMS

*So, understand the Light
(He answered), and make
friends with it.*

—Poimandres

1.

In green dark pounce on her musk
lock & roll with her, go
goat the bitch, make the ledge,
jump it

white ribbons streaming upwards

— * —

make yourself up into earth
thru roots to words that signify
beginnings, space to place your circle in

heal & bind, make all work renew

— * —

Dark earth of damp woods
a bird brings forth light, brings
the sun in its beak, pulls night away
as a lover gently pulls the bedsheet down
to reveal love to the morning

2.

Circling cloud shadows infant acre.
Black patterns on first bud, new leaf
oily with birth. A brace of crow
discuss attack in the white exploding cherry tree.

Heavy arm on the farmer's belly O hot
plump moon bride moves to him and he, asleep, to her.
They awaken laughing. A festival

— * —

the cloud stopped by an angel who halves it.
Sunburst deluge

3.

Broken, pinned, its wings stretched on rude board:
dead black bird hunted down (done) by
Archon's men.

Bird-seekers, I said: Phoenix! Not you,
dumb old noble crow puzzled at this end,
a royal shaft humming in your heart.

What to do before your carcass stiff with death
& empty; realize how bones hold form
& keep feathers from falling off?

Nine in the party march with rook to board.
The grey sky marks their red uniforms
burn the eye. Their boots creak like boats

— * —

new wound opens its eye to rain

old men after me with leeches & powder
don't they see
I bear the mark with pride

TISHAH B'OV / 1952

Tishah B'Ov (the 9th day of the Jewish month Ov) is a day of mourning, during which Jews fast and bewail the destruction of the Temple and Jerusalem.

—Schauss: *Guide to Jewish Holy Days*

Marty was the first holy man I knew. He was a pale seventeen-year-old rabbinical student at the Yeshivah University. I spent Tishah B'Ov with Marty in 1952. We fasted, went to shul, then walked on the Rockaway Boardwalk, looking at the sea, watching sea gulls strut & scavenge in the sand.

Months later, we strolled thru a State Park. Marty was profoundly silent. I was silent too, hoping a Revelation would come into his sacred skull & I'd be there to hear it & humbly transcribe it for all mankind.

We came to an empty playground & sat upon swings, swaying back & forth, our toes gliding through the dirt.

Beyond the trees I could hear sounds of trucks and cars passing over the highway. Our silence was so huge, I could hear twigs move, I heard my blood moving through my veins. Finally Marty spoke.

—Do you see those cars going down the highway?
I nodded.
—Do you see those trees?
—Yes.
—Do you know what?
—No, Marty, what? I asked him, keeper of the Great Secret Key to numbers, letters, & God.
—Bullshit, said Marty softly. —They're all bullshit. The trees, the cars, the leaves, your sneakers. Bullshit. Everything is bullshit.

— * —

Grey Rockaway sky, is this it? Twilight
low tide, wicker chairs rolled home by the wind
vanishing into shadows into rooms
through kitchens into a bedroom, a bed & there
immediate death

O Lord O Elohim my heart
will go to You when I grow old
heavy with sorrow having spent Summer
in a parked car's dark feeling
beneath her silk garments, smoking
cigarettes, fearing nothing

tribal grief soothed by great unblinking seas
which part before the atoning eye
why mourn?
why blacken my horned head with *kippah*
stipple my brain with *Mishna*
burden my face with pious beard?

Tradition is energy
and will in time reshape my face
as I in time release its shadows
sending them into Your Light.
O Shaddai, your endless sea doth start & end in me
& I spill it into new life
it wets my work, flows into all points.
I seek and serve You as I can, as I will, as I'm able.

– * –

To shut my eyes & awaken years later
in a yellow stucco room. Green
leaf shadows, currents of air,
move across thin curtains.
Feel a cool breeze & look down
dazzled by new white sheets.

OYEZ! (DECEMBER 1965)

In hope I offer a fire-wheel,
    12 stars a-sparkle on the black
well waters, jasmine & rose leaves
    stolen from an albino hare
& 5 lily petals
    pilfered from the dove

Knowing stuff of tribute's only for the hand
    O Jesus what awakens the sleeping heart?
Off with my robes, roll my rings & coins down
    cobble, shave my head, set my flesh a-fire,
a star instinct follows?

    Light thru wound & wings break thru
my back, wings of light, wings of snow
    O Christos!
your four mirrors turn the fox blind,
    sight the mole, my face four times
broken in your light
    O Christ!
I seek sight beyond glass

    & offer up a fire-wheel. 12 stars
a-sparkle on the water's black disc,
    jasmine & rose leaves stolen from
an albino hare & 5 lily petals
    pilfered from the dove.

4.

From *The Dark Continent* (1967)

FOR ZAP THE ZEN MONK (1960)

Cold grove to grow top pot in.
Wet dew sops through sleepingbag.
Hibachi's rusty, crudded,
covered with dove shit, dung of cranes.

Wind tears down bamboo tent
and tender flesh bruises.
Only the mind hardens like ice
to crack and melt into a stream

touching roots (like nerve-ends)
closest to this dream of earth.

FOR LENNY BRUCE

All clowns arise in black gowns of law,
rise up, sing off-key and curse Heaven
throughout Eternity

Died for us. His weakness
our weakness. Habit
shuts the eye. Afraid
to die, afraid of dark,
afraid of light, of pain
not pain but fear of it,
he quit. Dead on bathroom tile.
Photo in the morning paper.
Recomposed in morphine snow static.

Old ones and kabbalists ghosting through
Brooklyn's ghettos, talking with goats
and God, living through endless books
consumed by the Law

World in world, head in head, a reel
of fishing line linked with cosmos, all
after the Whale, the Grail, the truth
driven mad with questions, embalmed
in a million miles of recording tape

finally quit it in Hollywood on a bathroom floor

FOR CELINE

Dead the day Hemingway blew his brains out in Ketchum

Céline died of contagious poison
crawled on hands and knees
to puke it all out on our plate

like Artaud, Rimbaud
he chucked up his gripes
barfed back at the dogs

sour frog doc had icy blue eyes
WW I shrapnel in his brain
electric sander hits a knothole
every second

disorder prophet
healer, one with people
arguing with history's phantoms
confer with bomb-throwing shadows
framed in cinema alleyways

upstairs, a radio's too loud
a man pounds his skull against plaster
a sniper loads up
a man bangs his wife's head open with iron fryingpan
rushes her howling to the Doc's pigpen salon
& Louis-Ferdinand swabs out the muck
sews her up and out she goes
hold to earth, fall into Atlantis
knock-down a half-pint of Absinthe

Céline was one with those whose hair grows
out of the heart into the head and onto the chin

Rumplestiltsken wolf-men
who see through the world
like worms in apples

died the day Hemingway blew his brains out
in a hunting lodge in Ketchum
watching a mountain range disappear

FOR HANK WILLIAMS

*—If I can't finish writing a song in ten minutes
it ain't worth the finishing,*
said Hank to a reporter.
A camera taking pictures for LIFE.

—I'll never get out of this world alive,
wrote Hank in a song bought by millions
sung for thousands at the Opry
published by Acuff-Rose Sales, Inc.
recorded by M.G.M. Records

flat-picking his D-28 backed up by
the Drifting Cowboys night after night
and during the days playing picnics
rallies, gala supermarket openings

—There's no dreams but bad ones,
Hank told Audrey who told her lover
who told the doctor who couldn't heal him

places no longer places
velocity of faces
died at 29 of an overdose
kindly rocked to sleep
in the backseat of his Cadillac
en route to a concert
New Year's Day 1953

FOR JACK SPICER

I'm out of touch with stars. The bar's
closed. We go groggy down Grant
to Columbus to the Park to somebody's parked car.
One of us says, Let's go to Ebbe's. Ebbe says,
Sure, why not, let's go. We're gone
piled in the back seat breathing wine on windowpanes.
Seven Years ago. Tonight

you're gone. Maybe that night it was
Marco who fell back on the bush.
We left him there to sleep it off.

5.

From *Round the Poem Box: Rustic & Domestic
Home Movies for Stan & Jane Brakhage* (1969)

FANFARE

For my teachers who forgot the plot & left it up to me
in this dark green brown silt clay fern web mudhole time of
day
(dog tags jingle outside the door)

The lesson turns against the mouth
the mouth upon the glass
floor of your heart
part of her breast tip drips
juice like bent prick done & spent
white drop of 300,000 faces

For my teachers & for the dogs in the woods
& Nefertiti lady grace with deer eyes
canoe-ribbed greyhound sleeps on our sofa

ELECTION DAY TV

Today we lost it
  not like watching Gibson
drop it, instead it's
  Nixon
shit-faced before us.

Outside the window,
rain beads succulents

Watch the new President smile
  rat tails slip back into
his mouth's uneasy corners.

Pat's steelwool peroxide hair, peaceful
  cat-smile, states it's more fun
being a Winner. Eats alligator
  heart for breakfast in their
Waldorf Astoria suite.

THE ARGUMENT: 1

A tough night. Owls & a nightmare
hawk tried breaking thru the bedroom window.
I heard their wings slam against the glass,
the clack of their beaks.

—But what of it? she asks out of sleep
broken by my poking. —What if the bedroom's
filled with birds real or imagined?
Go back to sleep.

THE ARGUMENT: 2

—Oh, you, she hollers—with your books
on shelves, your poems in folders:
words, words, words, like high tide
fill up your room, fill up the house.
No wonder I nod-out before TV
waiting for you to come sing me a song
satisfy my needs, give me a moment
out of your time. No wonder.

SONNET: 3

The mouth falters letting go of words
it can't taste or see & I
falter with them tumbling on you
falling on our mattress filled with rubber
foamed with air. Okay,
let the voyeur have us too
in his eyes, see us thru
binoculars, from rooftop or treetop
watch us in our moment with shut eyes.
The weld of coming fills this space
the distance between any of us.
For a moment we are all lovers.

NATURE POEM

Absurd. We talk of progress.
My hair falls out all over the place.
Into a bowl of mushrooms. What a mess.
How much have I swallowed?
Yet I let my hair fall. Ha.
See how man copes with nature.

— * —

My teeth shrink, rot
into nerve-end threads.
The enamel turns upon itself.
I allow my teeth to disappear.

— * —

My face falls into place.
Wrinkles work into folds, crack
& sag over my bent jaw.
I allow my face.
My tongue dries like a prune.
Too much air.
I let my tongue evolve.
Soon I'll be an old man.
Many years ago I was a baby.
Absurd. We talk of progress.

ANOTHER ARGUMENT

Tough short-order cook bangs her hand on the hard-wood
        counter,
says

No more of this shit. I'm more than human,
I'm a woman!

Early morning workers watch her
over thick coffeecup rims & let her
work it out.

She flips a pancake to the ceiling
& hopes it sticks there forever
along with the bacon-fat stars.

I'M GREEDY. I LIE. I CHEAT. I'M AFRAID OF FAILURE. IS IT TRUE I ALSO STEAL?

Gimme all of it

what good's sunset
it burns out smog light
plaster city murder warfare echo
street debris of real unmoving bodies
can't be stuffed fast enough into exploding graveplots
overtime furnace engines streak God's mouth

What good is sunset?
instead I grow a brute forehead, squashed nose
cower in the basement
TV night & day
watch the world move out of sight
into regulated cataclysm
taste damp fart earth sight
bright cold morning no sleep again
watching darkness grind my skull bowl down
eyebrows heavy with fear

Gimme it all, everything

Thick mutant thumbs scoop out brass trays
in cash registers, strangle banks with number
ribbons, feed hungry rat teeth green lips
gobbling money while the little lady (bless her)
strapped to bed knits green sweaters to cover my head
hide my face from the kids off to school

What good is sunrise?

breaking over tired wounded brain forest
mirror light ricochets off glass
spirit writhes, dies
stuffed & shocked with mirrors
babbling in terror:

I lyre I cheep I steel

Murder Rape Frayed

chained splayed on spirit-wheel spokes
roll away into Infinity

God help me

6.

From *Yesod* (1969)

In memory of Asa Benveniste

RETURN

Let us see, is this real
let us see, is this real
this life I'm living?

Gods who dwell everywhere
let us see, is this real
this life I'm living?

—Pawnee War Song

Off at dawn a seeker in the chill
wearing easy clothes: soft black Italian
hiking boots, well-worn sweater, Levis, wool socks.
The same reasons: my world not clearly mine
I think too much about illusion, power's art,
media's hieroglyphic maya.
The clan, my brood, blank before TV
watching for themselves. Ghosts
squashed in loud homes, brain wires
cut with abundance.

Mountain peak above ancient redwoods
centuries old. Morning haiku. Whistle into
mist. No bird answers back. Fat chance.

Jackcheese sandwich in my paper sack,
an orange, some sunflower seeds,
traditional kick-off hike pack.
It's an easy dance to follow the fool.

Scrubjay squawks
its mouth stuffed with worms.
My breath on the compass circle.

FOR RAYMOND CHANDLER

One dawn it happens.
Fading star of vision.
Pack up, backpack down
old Trusty Mountain, old
crusty cave of comfort
feathered with eagle down.
All my poems are fading comicbooks
stashed, sent packing downstream.

One dawn it happens.   Simple.
Star of vision fades.
Everything gets faster.
The movie sped-up, run backwards
or forwards. Enter city gates
quicker than a cartoon, strip off
pack, change into quick getaway sneaks,
stay-press easy-wash slacks, shirt,
wallet, car keys, notebook, bankbook,
coins, checks, cigarettes, calling cards.

Elevator to my office. A brass key
opens the door. Must of trapped time
behind shut windows, drawn blinds. Faces
on file. The works. Stored in fire-proof
iron cases. Open the windows, snap on the fan,
put a rubberband around the mail. My pistol
on a peg, oiled, ready in its hand-made
rawhide holster. Light up a Lucky.
The phone rings. Back in business. Exhale.

7.

The Eyes, the Blood (1973)

The effect of this attitude was to place the Jew beyond the pale of human society. The Church enhanced Christian aversion for the Jew by its policy on intermarriage. Not content with prohibiting it "because there can be no fellowship between a believer and an unbeliever," it condemned such a union with all the weight of threatened penalty at its command, not excluding excommunication and the death sentence, as adultery.

— * —

". . . since coition with a Jewess is precisely the same as if a man should copulate with a dog."

— * —

All intermarriage between Jews and non-Jews is forbidden by Jewish law and invalid, unless the non-Jewish partner has been first converted to Judaism. The child of a mixed or an invalid marriage is considered to have the faith and status of the mother. Thus a child of a Jewish father and a non-Jewish mother is regarded as non-Jewish while that of a non-Jewish father and a Jewish mother as Jewish. Since intermarriage is invalid, no divorce is necessary to dissolve it.

1.

My mother of the blue
Anglo-Saxon eyes,
my father of the brown
eyed Jews, fused
and formed my exile
here on earth,
this year turning into next year
while the turn of my songs goes out
to renew source, ancient sorrows
become newly-cast. The sky
swept of grey clouds

turns into a blue dome
unmarked by birds or Monarch gold.
My mother's eyes hold the Bolinas sky
as in my father's eyes
the mud of its roads.

— * —

Her father stood 6 foot 5
and in the old photo
stands between railroad ties
holding a sledge-hammer
cap aslant, blue-eyed.
My father's father
short and stocky
holds me to the Kodak,
face shaded by the brim of
a pearl-grey fedora.
I adored him for what he brought
of Russia and Jews.
Chain-smoking Old Golds,
he saw in my eyes dark roads
three sons came to America to travel.
He could never accept it,
an intellectual, America
he could care for less.
An exile, he knew the mark,
could read it instantly in the eyes of others.
A light like pain's spark
sudden in Cain's eyes.

My mother's mother
ran off with a lover and left her
to her widowed mother.
Tough, orderly, a gritty Yankee,
decent, clean, everything in place.
Blue-eyed *shiksa*, my father's servant.
Aunts and uncles whispered the Christ curse
in her blood mixed in the children's blood.
A contamination.

By Law we were neither here nor there.
Dispossessed, exiled at birth by blood.
They held her to blame for all of it.
Dachau, Belsen, Buchenwald.
In secret rage
she bleached her brown hair wheat-blonde
and ladled-out chicken soup into their bowls.

~ * ~

My mother's blue-eyed brother, 6 foot 2, blonde
crewcut, Lieutenant, U.S. Navy,
on leave, visiting our Brooklyn flat,
battle-ribbons flashing on his dark blue chest.
Pink-cheeked, he entered our twilight livingroom,
sat on the piano bench, hitting a note randomly
as he talked and listened. We passed around
a snapshot of the submarine he worked on
in Florida's green mystery where old Jews go
to mock *Pardes* under the sun, pseudo-Riviera
rocked in wicker chairs pushed along by young
Puerto Ricans in white uniforms, roasting
on the brilliant beaches. Skin turning parchment
brown, Torah scroll brown my father's skin turned
sunning on the stoop. Cars moving constantly
over Linden Boulevard.

2.

Each family to its mysteries whispered through the
        branches.
A cousin in Syracuse with dark brown eyes
died the day before her 18th birthday.
A rare blood disease.
She had a pale narrow face framed in
famous long black hair reaching her knees.
Her mother's pride,
the hair grew as the girl grew,
braided into one huge braid the day she died,
carried into the grave, her triumph.

She looked like a Russian countess in the photo
passed around by Grandmother Sarah.
It runs in the family, in the blood,
in the eyes, the diluted tribe of Judah.

— * —

Dark-eyed cousins.
Lonnie from Minneapolis
came to 'Frisco after highschool with his buddy Ivar.
One night they climbed the Golden Gate Bridge
and sat across from each other, each
to his own tower, kings in iron castles
swaying high above a new domain.
Sparkling Oakland, shimmering 'Frisco
Marin's dark forests. He showed me
thick suede work gloves torn through
the palms, the edges burnt away,
pulled back like a row cut in earth for seed,
where he slipped going down
grabbing cables on both sides to brake the slide.

3.

Her tall blond blue-eyed men all came to California,
straight and proud they stood and each one of them
remembered by my great-grandmother, a century old
and still going. Broke her hip at 87
painting the outside of her home. A Freeway
benedicts her frontyard with shadows.
3 blocks from L.A. County Jail.
She took me to its steps when I disobeyed her.
Until 13 she sent me a subscription to
the National Geographic Kodachrome world,
world she saw, a world of postcards where
pink well-fed Americans all over the globe
stand straight and self-reliant beneath
glossy blue skies. Blue the light
breaking through her blue eyes. Radiance
of new shores, plains and railroads.

Marks in the land. Carved-out places
where rightfully secure her forebears spawned
blue-eyed generations of men and women
forever heroic in bright postcard light.

— * —

An orderly home.
In a glass-doored bookcase stand leather albums of officers
and gentlemen who fought and perished in the Civil War; fat
scrapbooks of family history: luncheon programs, photo-
graphs, daguerrotypes. Lodge meeting announcements,
calling-cards, concert programs, meetings, news metal-typed
black on dried-out newspaper turning gold, glued onto black
scrapbook pages, photos held by black triangles. She keeps
all evidence she can find of her blue-eyed men
who came to make it new, renew it right
reduce the space extended from shore by green
timber vistas of the New World, hills
whose verdure dipped into dark forests
edging into shapely female plains
turning into painted deserts into primordial mesas
transformed in bayous feeding into wide rivers
roaring into waterfalls filling lakes
that hold reflections of great mountains
and all of it, before that moment,
unmarked or tracked by the blue-eyed presence.
No wonder natives thought them divine.
How to deny ownership's sure white stride?
They broke the seal of America's shores
and where they wounded earth
they closed the wound with cities
that spread as root-systems through the landscape.
White rightness wed with the pure goal of progress
linked by telegraph and steam engine and automatic
rifles.
No questions asked. There was work to do.
Bridges, doors, connections to make new.
To cramp it all into zoos and cells
men and animals spend lifetimes breaking out of.

Lovelace. I saw it as cotton doilies
on stiff armchairs in great-grandmother's livingroom.
White lace *mantillas,* white choirboy collars.
Doily dress of mandallas worn
over the dark sinned Toltec hooker.
16 years old, her skin webbed white,
cunt hairs, beard curls, loop and spring
through the weave. Mid-noon *fiesta.*
Her bare feet on carpets of time-dark flowers
break the tomb-quiet of the livingroom.
I throw silver dollars at her feet,
aluminum pennies. She does a split
and juice from her slot sparkles a snail trail
on petals of the rugs shadowy blossoms.
Tequila guzzled straight from the bottle while
tortillas cook on the griddle. The old
blue-eyed lady's stomach would turn against our smells.
Love   Lace
A dress on the Mexican whore
who stood in the doorway whispering
Love, love, I got it!
Love, love, I got it.
See, I got it. You want it? Take it,
come on my great-grandmother's bed.
Sheets newspaper brittle, everything
stinks of sachets. Gutstring guitars
outside the window, *mariachi* trumpets, thump of
the *gitaron,* boogie-woogie, V-J Day
out of a metal Arvin radio.
I push into her, she milks me,
a frenzy. No matter, she won't let go
and covets Lemoge teacups in teakwood stands.
No matter she's a dream I tangle with
in sheets, look out to see two orange trees
in the backyard, no leaf misplaced, boughs
kept trim by the old lady, *Lovelace.*
A space where stars burn through black

to create a lace illusion not unlike
the common household doily covering
every stiff stuffed chair in her livingroom.

4.

Grandmother Sarah re-married at 90
and went back to Europe on her honeymoon.
No more hotel rooms with milk and sweet
butter on the windowledge. No more
Workmen's Circle monthly ghost-quest
for Grandfather Benjamin who came to America
to become a tailor and died on my bed in Brooklyn,
cancer spreading terrible wings
within his body. Grandmother Sarah
always a good touch for music and money
playing mandolin with thick fingers
as sun set over Broadway parkbenches
thirteen floors below. Minor-key
schmaltz, grief, pain and pride
of time and tribe, making music
for her grandson, a wolf
in the room's only chair,
listening to Poland, Jews in Paradise.

When the music left her hands,
Grandmother Sarah told stories of the village,
a river ran through its green and golden fields.
Young men intrigued by her dark beauty
called her The Gypsy. But now, she'd say,
the village is no more, the young men are dead,
bombed off the map by Nazis during the last war.

~ * ~

What do I know of journey,
they who came before me
no longer here to tell it
except baggage of old papers

bound up and found in library stacks.
History's crying makes it all vague.
Was it myth we all came here to be?

What do I know of journey,
I who never crossed the seas
into the USA alchemy, no longer
anyone's dream of home.
Their great great grandchildren
jump state's ship, drown in void
Torah's too late to warn of.
Here *tohu* is *bohu*, America
another *pogrom*, another camp
more subtle and final than all
Hitler's chemists could imagine.
Home, *ha-makom*, no longer hope.
It holds light reaching back
from eyes watching Asians and Blacks
die on TV. We restore the shore
and our dream is gone. It
mixes into shadows growing tall behind us.

What do I know of journey,
they who came before me kept
what they left but now are gone.
Invisible shells cast off
in flaming hair arise
orphans of collapsed Shekinah
caught between earth's end
and heaven's end and what do I know
of journey, I a child when children were
murdered waiting on lines with mother and father
gone in gas or the flash of A-Bomb *ain-sof*
squinted at in movie-theatres.
Ancients sit on stoops too tired to mourn
turning inward to blood rivers
mourning lost *shtetls.*
They cannot take me with them
and I cannot bring them back
and what do I know of journey

who never spoke their language.
The old ones are dead or dying
and what is left desires less and less
and what is less is what is left
and children run off screaming
Elohim Elohim!
into freeways filled the starlight of cars

CODA

My father was a clown
my mother a harpist.
We do not forget
how close to death love leads us.

I can not forget my father
crying in the uncomfortable chair
in a Long Island Railroad car.
His first and only son unable to turn
or run from a father's public grief.

My mother crying on the kitchen floor
a carving knife she couldn't use
against her flesh. Black metal
cast away. Broken
I do not forget

from these parts a music was once made.
She at the piano, he at the cello.
Late afternoon rehearsal. Slow
removal of light from the livingroom.

Discomfort between father and son
as in each other was the other
neither could forget.

The smells of her body in nylons
undergarments, buckles. The scar
across her belly. Dark fold of Death
the Angel's touch.

I do not forget
it starts in the blood and ends in the eyes.
A Bible impossible to read.
The rabbi I turned away from.
Kittens murdered in the garage
hurled against the walls.
Sensual hips of my sisters.

He died in Hollywood. Nobody there
to say Kaddish.
His common-law wife
a Christian Scientist
insisted no music be played.

My children will never know my father.
My mother will not see nor bless my family.
I do not forget that from these parts
a music was once made.
I heard it as a child.

— **BOOK TWO** —

1.

Arrows

♦

'Eros'
backwards
'sore'

Arose, he rose, his sore stem
bud pricked bush flower array
pointing to love's floral glossary

stalks habit her blossom he roots for
again, arise love flower
making vocabulary

what's left hive as mirrors to re-arrange light
unthinking blinking cock engorged divining
rod roots up its twitchy energy antenna
imagines love or God whatever we root for

◆

Postcard: pale blue synthetic
fabric crotchless silk screened
brief comes in today's mailbox

◆

need for a whip her mouth eats
inside a dream of blind enclosed rite
dream skin eat it beat it
partners forward Christ
love down on its knees
two do it apart

◆

language invents heaven
watch her hands unzip your fly
and look up

what deeds divine
words wont illumine

halved by mercury
is anything clear here?

naked ankle
sphincter lets go
shatters water

◆

Arose a rose
arrows soar
a row of roses

◆

who follows flows easily
love's oils break and enter
love's hive lights alive

who flows falls easily
slides in slo-mo grace
sensational

◆

Nazi leather riding crop
French maid singly crazed
debasement Polaroid
mote-room breasts
Willendorf sheath
sheer black sheen
spike glazed heels
belts and buckles
wide-hipped Kali
tweezers and paddles
diapers candle-wax
chains manacles
ball squeezing harness hoist
sandpaper cock cowl
tape-loop Muzak
mini-cam on tripod

◆

power against powerlessness
bland voyeur removes his hat
before unzipping sliding into
distance close-up reverie eyes shut
through everything

◆

fingernails dig into palm meat
matinee pick-up idyll sucked
tongue-torn roots

here to sing it in wings of roses
wild wide chrysanthemums
yellow ebony red lilacs dark
papyrus dust green fennel coil

◆

any body anywhere an eye cocks
through a hole in plaster board
quarter machines confession screens
right or wrong it's a rite two do
maestro, maestra pee into awe slave
mouth yaws open for work cellophane
glazed magazines glisten priced like cocaine

◆

impact barrier threshold boundary
what enters what leaves what appears what's left
what doesn't stay

romance dream codes glyphs eye
beyond page shapes nothing but desire
anoint warm oil spreading infusion
stain mesh brain tiers weep
face and hair slippery white webbing
shapes suggestive idea image detached
attached to watching surface flight
shiny moves glisten sparkling teeth
curve of thick red lower lip tongue
on wordless vein heat of unwritten
outside within

◆

master discourse master matrix
the teaching aims to cleave and core the veiled book
hierarchy hands dig in pull out black
blood hunks of torn language
roars in those climbing pillars
reassert mastery rules occult authority

◆

stick pins in your dick on the phone
I want to take your cock away by Phone!
Cock & Ball Torture Nipple Training Mistress
Sybil Fone Fantasy

each expired phoneme rims page with uncaught song
untied slaves drive home
warm milk TV trays moth in a box
grab raw bird red neck cranes up
flight to weep alone in after mask

2.

Bakelite

◆

The promise replaces the premise. Momentarily eternal, the
premise is promise.

A thick glass ball rests upon a black hard rimmed base.
      Inside,
in the snow, the 1939 New York World's Fair Trylon and
Perisphere.

Material, style, compromise, limits. Unrealized future,
      amnesia,
appearances, disappearances. Style

The moment, the era, erased, embraced. Style remains an
unpeopled world reflected in things re-told as history.
      Remains.

The premise of freedom, of invention, binds to thingdom an
unpeopled world of desire announcing impossible
      kingdoms
inexplicable as wireless, occult.

1.

adjustable aluminum ring from Cheerios
whose eyepiece pierces energy's heart
atomic sparks, trapped Luria on display

1945 toy, shining shroud
children stare into darkened rooms.

2.

curved, heavy, grooved, metal tone-arm
chocolate fork onto flat iron platter
circling music out of speaker web
lacquer maple bracketry
vacuum tubes of Phantom City

wrote without dictionary
listened without reference
music of itself in itself in circles
immediately history

3.

round unfrosted halo above inventor head
Eureka
dog's victor leaps through theremin chromium hoops
loops of Mesmer, Od, Orgone, Frank R. Paul lights
bubble through underground Gothams
Veidt aloft Bauhaus edges
Metropolis brass pneumatic glass tubes
Western Union vials of atomic colas
animate death sleeping beneath silk
envelopes of cinema geography ghosts
Plexiglas towers what's the hour shutting-down
the end of number, humbug

4.

face eaten by Art Deco mirrors below the Ladies' Room
hive thriving in honey of light
pink bowled death network masking each face
the silver veil devotion Hollywood
creche aerodynamic red-orange radio
Constance Bennett's profile looking away from above

5.

nickle-fed automatic food in bowed glass ripples
braced in brass chrome turrets/towers of beef pie
pickled beets glazed carrots/dense bran muffins on
thick white plates/tiered row after row food apartments
we read descriptions of food browsing Horn & Hardart
spouts coffee cream ribboned pasteurized sterilized
infinite immaculate

6.

coiled thrill, illusion to possess to own to imagine power
brilliant back panel of box code matched to de-code disc
sit in rite dark, green dial back-lit scribe messages
grimoire, win the war against Japan

an oasis for Tonto, cardboard construct
map of gold mines fold 100 times fits into ring's secret
     chamber

singer of blissful grain guide me up epiphanal ladders

7.

world of heavy objects, superior weight
durable iron toys, paint-flecked, lead, thick
aluminum, ore of permanence, gravity of goods
good old says of goods the post-war shift to
Lucite, plastic, aerated aluminum black and white
magnetic terriers dance into and out of
mummy's sarcophagus
thinning out into weightlessness
ineffable, disposable, endlessly karmical

8.

holograms, radio voices, forms inside secular Gothic metal
     vault
each vacuum tube a centurion speaking of strangers
familiar timed cycle enclosing borders regulating tide
     of goods
alluring waves touchable nouns abundance of plurals
     entrancing

9.

have asked you not to enter the border where the door is
     drawn
and the manic rabbit breaks through
devours a heart of feathers

asked you to turn away so I may reassemble the trick
        meant to
amaze

forget I'm inept I can't remember
which utopia each untutored move alludes to

there I've done it, the drawing's done
the rabbit a triumph of fury and blood
a disarray ready for the micro-wave

10.

how could I wonder beyond the page of pulp curves
        bearing scars
of inked desire, utopian forms, sensual contours, thick
impenetrable windows where helmeted people sit observing
leisure, Tarot disced metropolis, cellophane insight eternal
soft warm bread, spongy page of penicillin cure me

11.

"Mary Had a Little Lamb" carved by Edison
Peter Goldmark's grooves sound back through us out of us
beyond us fraternities, miracles invented in consort with
        voices
phantoms immortal Caruso racketing rocketing at 78 r.p.m.
a promise, a perfume, how to begin to own vapor
death in circles, the machine breaks down, lights burn out

fast-pouring brain sugar deckling flat plains
denatured flour discs live anywhere forever
glisten behind brown gas-bronzed glass panel
kitchen technocrat gazes watching natural foods
arise construct music by Kostelanetz

12.

erotic future forms, volute, circumcised
vaginal mall, perfect torsos leisure dream strolls
flexible supple arise to entwine Lucite innards
tram lights push commuters through travel wheels to

suburban palaces layers luxury pillows
drugged petal mulch lunch seizes power dreamer
sink into memory glades into forms of containment
hives their clones thick honey-gold porthole
open fire caught in Plexiglas ribboned phalloi
inside labial formulations Muzak embedded jewelry
plague escalators, formal teeth, Ophelia's garments
hover over and out clunky mike Buck clicks off

13.

Museum of Science & Industry, ground floor, Rockefeller
        Center
trigger-finger stuns lights networking countryside and city
tableaux behind store-window glass
repeatable illuminations each time a button's pushed down
bombadier for progress

tiny dreams of electricity
of work beyond all need for effort
wire our veins enweb our world thrumming
held behind glass, watch it work

chips talk ghost, formal, repeatable
slave-class wired from spare parts
avarice through facade costume ball for each
stalled clan, our rites, friezes
freeze-framed across pyramid walls

                — * —

restless poetry acts in between lights tense wires Happy Day
ski-mask oracle glowing somnambulists loop the world
together round as a Peace pin stuck in old tie-dyed headband
worn in Year of the Barricades

slip into sleep how gentle Gore-Tex goose-down larva fed by
Kodachrome fluids fuels tooled silk cap on skull dome cork
green steam jam it back down the chakras locking sitting
people fix pelvis into a wedge of rock

soft glass curved breasts abstract nipple cones coated interi-
or face-mask molded deathmask beaded sweat ciphers heat
steaming neon eye rims

watching without waiting filled with digital display unscrolled
hour after hour moment after moment products objects names
brands bandsaws laser-teeth high-tech surgery stipples each
neuron melds down into the air forms evaporate return
renewed

14.

"The 14-Ton Giant Underwood Master Typewriter Operating
Daily At The New York World's Fair 1939"

"The Singing Tower of Light. Westinghouse Building."

"Bridge of Tomorrow"

" 'The Impossible' In Spectacle Over Fountain Lake. Amuse-
ment Zone, New York World's Fair, 1939."

— * —

"Wall Decorations 'Painted' By Changing Colored Lights
"Houses Built Flush To Property Line—No Windows Needed
"Air-Conditioner—Electrical Discharge Removes Dust Particles
"Rooms Lighted By Artificial Sun Lamps
"Radio Newspaper
"Theatre Entertainment On Home Screen
"Temperature Controller—Refrigeration For Food and Heat For
House Supplied By Same Machine"

—L. Warrington Chubb
Director of Research
Westinghouse Electric & Manufacturing

— * —

vocabulary bends a poised leap over the edge

working same jambs together

quickly filmic
door's gone in blast of light
eclipse the point
duck cameras
answers, dive into a pool of first
available water

15.

losing the measured drone of authority's poem
kidnapped by childhood to a tomb of rooms papered with
        letters
child high striving to touch ceilings
seeing nothing black ink reach up recite
each letter discover America

16.

savoir oh how we danced on light we'd bled
we wanted a world palm stuffed plain splayed outward
to edges of dusk demented
its ululating sensualismo surrounds our bond
fevered tentacles of lithography silver circles
inscribed inner band of sigils heal
the bowed head apple-scented source of fury
source of peace signal bends wave fractures
against chromium towers iron glass impervious
bleed cartoon blood all over sidewalks crowing
crowd noises watchers cameras traffic

17.

they can fall off the rails into garbage below
tear away paper masking glass from paint
one's fat—large for his age—
the other fits correct clothes
they're friends
scavenging a house in process
empty on weekends
open for their anger

18.

who does light address, where do the words connect?
it's not enough to sit typing flow into darkness
pulse blip glyphs assume literacy
while everywhere, even in closed ears
radios and tapedeck insistently hammer
the building of Atlantis

who's silent in wood pulp weave?
noise pulls reader inside skin
moving automata, bottom beat
over-bassed, under foot, shaking floor
earthquake regulating machines

it's more presence, this present
stacked up in shelves, boxed
in warehouse towers, stuff
crisis abounding metastasizing
shrink-wrapped sparkling vessels brilliant
light fractured dazzle
aisles sound-surround wordless
ritual music

suddenly used, broken-into
new vanishes
micro-second of its revelation—

19.

often no world beyond that

often foul smells of skunk raining down
subtle mist from ceilings

often a fawn assembled in Taiwan
last hummingbird lights before dark
and arising rates

often not much moves through or beyond
the formal poem stuck in its violent grid

flat nasal eros anonymous salesman at the other end
of phones answered by machines

desire tics ripe type plied plaited
weave of transcontinental digitalizing copper wires
state of messages

often TV Superbowl Sunday no matter
how paper hides its vegetable origin
light scours the steamed flower blue

20.

zoned magic world words image
nimbus halo consuming clues
to be consumed by frenzy TV rays
mutable mutated plea-bargaining
huckster shyster shlockmeister
motivational researchers scrape
nubbed nerve-end edges O fully needy now

desire hear electric passion sizzle longing
for connection release not just Bakelite but
Nylon, Aluminum, they would
end need fill yearning
close complete break the circle

deep hunger buried no food reaches hunger's ghost
pull skin's pink inside threaded to veneered intestines
unrolling miles of process around imagined planets
never reaching itself never ending awakened book
uroboric hopelessness
no elegant style desiring desire what's imaginable
without turning the page zapping the channel

come now this isn't meant this doesn't mean anything
lines of weaving woven into wood death
ink dust flecks chips dark crease shadowy valley signatures
jammed into bug-sucked bookspine

each phoneme a threshold
each inked mark a barrier
a dividing line a loop

Everything had to appear to endure; these were Depression
goods which were then trimmed, cut-back, rationed to func-
tion as War goods

Guy in a cheapo three-piece suit, sits in a chair, hat on knees,
turns away from *Opportunity* ("The Magazine of Salesman-
ship"); Claudette Colbert, a genie to beat the blues, muse of
subscriptions, opens the magazine. 500 firms need you! Who's
afraid of the big bad world wolf? Mr. Dithers eager to hire; Tom
Mix needs hands at Melody Ranch; tattoo the red blue eagle
on soft shoulder gristle, cover up the pox shot crater.

Industrial Moderne: electric clock in chromium-plated zinc
designed by Gilbert Rohde, 1934, without lightning bolts; run-
ning borzoi frozen in Lucite; streamlined locomotives embed-
ded in metal scrap-basket—there, spools of used-up typewriter
ribbons, black Medusa coils, sprung.

Black enamel ashtray, tubular frame, stained with nicotine lac-
quer; silver martini shaker, engraved verticals, horizontals;
modern is movement; he and she after a few watch the perfect
stranger enter glass doors from the sunlit garden, compulsively,
his yo-yo, large, ebony, amazing tricks, perhaps he's Filipino—

Sunroom Moderne, torchere floor lamps, upholstered chrome
tubular chairs, chrome tables, black dense lacquer top; her
eyes turn gray, her lips press an image on the black cold shine;
vermouth refrain, his mouth against her spine ridge at neck
base; lick salt, exhale gin

crackle-glass, reclining shiny white marble Egyptian-style
nude

21.

tropical fish jungle birds parrots cockatoos cranes flamingos
dogs borzoi greyhounds whippet thonged to beautiful women
in picture hats; German shepherds Kerry blues Boston bull ter-
riers Scotties; wirehaired terriers

decorations on glasses, ashtrays. serving trays, bowls, metal
boxes, canisters

panthers lions

Noritake: Japan-ware sold in five-and-dimes hand-painted flow-
er vases, incense burners, tiny glass figures, pitchers, pin-
cushions

modern Depression goods cocktail shakers coffee servers fan-
cy dishes buffet sets bright electro-plated chrome copper brass
with Catalin Bakelite accents

cobalt blue

zigzag triangular declinate patterns; waves Egyptian ziggurat
exaggerated fruit floral motifs vegetable cornucopia Moderne
style gods and goddesses Zeus Mercury Diana

new hidden fluorescent Lumalite indirect

22.

a moment hidden in a thing as if owning imagines retrieving
nostos—return(ing) home—*algos*—pain

an imaginary home hidden in the thing, an autobiography
self hidden in the thing apart from it, owning it, reading it,
remembering it, replacing it, hiding it, losing it, forgetting

each moment opening its counter myth, new story, history,
old is new/new is old, history is mystery/mystery is history,
a mint Big Little Book, *Chandu the Magician* inscribed by Bela
Lugosi, pristine, crisp, unopened box of Oxydol

plastikos, to form or mold substance of special molecular structure repeatedly softened by heat re-formed retaining shapeable quality, resiliant pliant in the heat the kiln of thumbs tongs of utility

fossilized resins amber animal protein: horn tortoise-shell shellac *gutta percha* from Malayan trees the appearance of rubber; rubber's plastic qualities but its elasticity places it in the category of elastomers; plastics natural or manufactured are defined as polymers: *poly* many *mer* part the companion ship of duplicity a Xerox indisgression replicating the whole whorl of the divine thumb into 8 x 10 posters stapled all over the neighborhood

— * —

"In 1907, Dr. Leo Baekland invented the first entirely synthetic plastic. (Because Celluloid and protein plastics are based on plant and animal substances, they usually are classified as semi-synthetics.) It was a thermosetting resin that he patented in 1909 under the name Bakelite. It was the material that, in a much more significant way than Celluloid, inaugurated the modern plastics industry. Baekland was a Belgian-born chemist of genius. Before concentrating on resins, he had invented and produced Velox photographic printing paper, which, in 1899, he sold to the Eastman Kodak Company for three-quarters of a million dollars. This considerable fortune left him free to pursue independent research for the rest of his life. Working in a small laboratory adjacent to his home in a fashionable section of Yonkers, New York, Baekland took up a problem that for years had challenged and defeated other gifted researchers: the creation of a thermosetting resin from the reaction of phenol (carbolic acid) with formaldehyde . . . Baekland was interested initially in developing a shellac and varnish substitute. However, he quickly realized

24.

a compound, a material, an apartness
solid irreducible nugget in the dumps
silent and resistant desiring its chains to be reshaped

stuff, an apartness, un-shape solid pulled from your
        burning
home
edges of streamlined promise broken
fused talmismanic lump held in the palm of her hand
attempts an inventory of all that was lost

3.

Monkey

♦

Into surrounding truth linked by noisy monkeys—zoo-trained
to dance around rock piles—grailed by iron railing grids—
barbed wire—

Later that night in meat's abuse—unexpected tacky scene—

Going back on the bus—she's sure the eye against the glass—
opening—was mine—a bubble looking beyond—spirit vapor—
storm warning—cloud packs speared by Dore glaciers—grim
Eskimos—bells and face paint—sweat—fracture lens—
eclipse—dark days—before film runs out—

Lost gods—goddesses—godlings—godlets—of airwave
wonders—ascending coils—other weights of light too spoiled
to sing of—

And we go to the Monkey Bar to dance—to smoke—drink er-
got nectar from Maria's garden of Allah—high on windswept
cardboard Sunset mesas somewhere near R.K.O. Mars—a wol-
fen coven seizing spores between gold—chromium—teeth—

An approach we face alone as the poem divides back to the
one writing it—I open my mouth before the hood drops—

Bruised before Yahweh—singing blues via crank-up
gramophone—sand-blasted disc—racket of decoded time—I
didn't want to pray: shawled and bound—twisting *tzitzit*
around my fidgety fingers—Nous abounding—surrounding
each atom—she sang—my head—heavy with inoperative
gears—cognitive ruts—stuck counting tiles below—wait for
needle to shatter inner circle which—when hit—trips platter's
end—

We all began variously—to unwind—

Wanted to be taken away—or beyond—or even to be here
now—awake to all of it—whatever's beyond it—within it—I
wanted the works—the lights—

Free of it all—the vocabulary bussing through white spaces—
dumbly served by life—fumbling thumb-index lexicon for new
ones—indeed a bumbler—a numb soul in ink—nibs and type—
dip cold edges into gray escalators—subway cars take me back
to arcane books—I wanted transformation—acts and arts of
reading—hurled back—in the grid of light broken by iron—
cross-wired—back on thick streets—human air—sacred struc-
tures propped-up—still secret—

In my monkey suit on Monkey Island—nobody knows whether
I'm awake or alive—I keep my trap shut—they see me as
scenery—backdrop kitsch—Rousseau—some barrio muralist
spraypaints day-glo—boulevard jades—sizzle pinks—lewd
palm fronds prod blue nylon skies—drunk volcanoes erupt dry-
ice trays—orange rind grog—Maraschino cartoon moons—
nose-down extra-long brown cigarette ferments in glass
ashtray—

Suave in my tux—I hop from table to plateau—a tightrope
walker through crowds—my thick palms—awake to the
warm—flash of silver trays—I bow—

In my monkey suit on Hollywood Boulevard—singing in the
rain—Kong gone wrong in spats—tails—top hat—a late night
movie—the god who is everywhere—a plurality of illusions—

"The monkey also wishes it had a straw coat"—worn in Basho's
warm rainfall—neon pellets stipple her eyelids—too stoned to
open—album-cover mouth moves over the song—eraphoned
into her gelatin skull—

To ape my monkey bent—a strange range of events—finds
me—tail-less—estranged on real mythways—anonymous
mark—monkey-shining blur of signs—wall-leaning hustlers
hawk codes—offer coke crack or junk—white way mystery
powders—cooked or tongued—or tubed up the nose—fired into
veins—kingdom bullets—lift the crown—beyond form—
closure—

For a moment—this monkey—slumps down—low—erased—

118

How to know nothing—unknown—leap up—barefoot—throw
back their garbage—fondle pecker—pull at it—

Gelobt seist du, Niemand.
Dir Zuleib wollen
wir bluhn.
Dir
entgegen.

All systems want out—even ones that worked

Playing at light's other side—skin tattooed with *sh'viti*—blue
and red—letter trees—her black fingertips touch—torn red
plastic fingernails—down his scholarly back—

The past you accomplish—becomes our future—otherwise, no
wisdom—merely armies in the Name nobody can pronounce—

Outside: footsteps are apples falling off the tree—cycles of
entering—retreating—what is the world we see—cycles of
seeing—where to go—when to leave

It's a real tree my words mistake for light.

4.

Pardes

In Memory of Edmond Jabès and Donald Schenker

◆

It's an old story—nobody believes it—everyone wants to know what it "means."

"Pardes is the symbolic and mystical garden in Kabbalah containing the supreme knowledge of the Creator and creation. It requires great courage to enter the Garden . . . The legend tells of the four Tanaim who entered the Garden: Rabbi Ben Azai, ben Zoma, Elisha ben Avuah, and Rabbi Akiva. Ben Azai gazed—died . . . Ben Zoma looked—lost his senses . . . Elisha ben Avuah cut trees down—became a heretic. Only Rabbi Akiva entered the Garden in peace and left the Garden in peace."

"Four persons—enter Pardes—orchard—study of theosophic speculations of—the Gnostic—concerning the nature of the Godhead, the process of Creation, the mystery of Evil . . . These were: Ben Azzai, Ben Zoma, Aher ('the other one'), and Rabbi Akiva. Ben Zoma—looked—died at an early age; Ben Azzai looked—became demented; Elisha ben Avuyah cut down the plants of Torah—became estranged from Judaism—and Rabbi Akiva alone—emerged in peace."

It's an old story—in an ancient language—translated in English—tells another story—nobody reads the same way—nobody knows its "real" meaning—everyone tells the story as if they knew something—

It is said: 4 men, tana'im, enter PaRDeS—3 return—

The Garden—Paradise—inward—as instructed—alive—before one's eyes—

In parable what's possible passes elsewhere—what's forgotten in dreams—remain—

Real or dream garden—paradise or arbor—four men dreaming as one—real as four—fictional—faceless—names—

An apparent stem or transparent tree—each branch—leaf—bud—a particular story—

We assume—four tana'im were there (where?)—nothing—no text—survives—it's a story others tell—for the first time—

If none wrote it—did anyone tell it? If anyone told it—who wrote it—what did they hear—what did it mean when meaning began—?

Scroll silent—meat planked into midrashim—tree beaten into straps of text—

Variants rarely waste words describing—names, nouns, verbs are the story—essential, what needs to be told—what happened without shadows—

We're told only what's seen—Ben Azzai sees—dies—
Ben Zoma sees—is "stricken"—
Ben Avuyah sees—uproots saplings—
Akiva "enters in peace/departs in peace"—but what does he see?
Whatever they "see" is not described—isn't told—

Four real or dream men enter bearing four names—and leave bearing five names—

How deliberate can the act of writing be when music out of tiny speakers constructs a counter lyric—?

For real or dream—men—enter with four names—leave with five names—

Elisha ben Avuyah—un-named—*aher*—"other"—anonymous—no longer with us—not a name—not in our presence—even when standing there—we refuse the name a minyan heard—on the 8th day carved into birth—flesh—Yesod—central as a name—

Azzai—Zoma—Avuyah—Akiva—
one—or four—enter the real—or dream-real—
garden—PaRDeS—paradise—orchard—
sacred—or secret—grove—
someone's backyard garden—a courtyard—a labyrinth—a
page—a name—erased—a word

What can be told will be told. What can not can not. What can
not be told will not be told. What can not be told will not be
told until it can be told. What can be told will be told.

— * —

The mystics—the poets—the rabbis—in the garden—strive—
tuned to beyond—an above—unattached from weights of
distraction—fly like an angel—yet unlike an angel—more moth
like to light—more light—

in flight—like an angel—soul like a moth—to light—more than
light—

blaze beyond likeness—

light—like its name—light—like it is—spelled—light—only the
word—light

light—unlike light—only the word—a name—
a substitute—a disguise—a mask—a ghost—

The four enter—what before—existed—only—as words
—describing a garden—
they recite Torah of the Garden—discourse—Talmud of
Flowering—listen to Akiva—his silence—

Layer by layer—the garden built—by his words—from black—
lightless—core—a seed of yud—stirs—in its sleep—

Black—lightless—plane—place of birth—nothing dies—
Blackness inside closed book—
Blackness—its word—its ink—

Akiva starts there—layer by layer—week after week—
They listen—to remember—
They remember—what they can—
They remember what they must—to enter—

Children finally able to speak—
They enter a room—day after day—week after week—a
teacher reads a line from the book—to remember—
Line after line—week after week—until—they know—
the book

They know the book before they learn to read its letters.
They know the book.

— * —

Optional—musk-woven—breezes—
wavering segments—four robed figures—
watch light—upon water—play

Four figures—light dismembers—
entered by gold—smudged—muscle—moving—
ibis legs—fishing

— * —

But—her story—
what would it tell—we kings—fathers of all—especially
language—

What would it tell—would it—tell—a tale—
we neither wish—nor want—

Four men enter a garden—the mother—*malkuth*—
seek birth—within—without—skull birth—
head babies—handed to women—to suckle—

Four men—woven skullcaps—fringed shawls—*kippah*—
tallith—shield—protects—head holes—babies—sprout
—out—of

But—her story—

Covered—awaits—weekly moment—face to face—in darkness
—Shekinah's wings—outstretched—bless life—streaming—
into her—twice-cursed—ark—

What does—her story—tell—we—kings—
fathers of all—but—especially—language—

— * —

The real garden in the backyard. On the page, a metaphor—
black and white blocks grow words—feed few—

Get-well postcard from Mei-Mei (*It's the Day for the Garden*)—
16th century Persian miniature—"an imperial copy of the
Divan of Anvari"—two turbaned men tend a garden—two ducks
swim atop a square tiled pool—divides picture in half—she
writes:

> "This highly cultivated garden of Akbar is
> a response to the birds return here, this week.
> The air was not thick and soft, particularly at
> sunset. Crocuses."

The prison garden at Vacaville—attended by inmates cunning
enough—lucky enough—to get the job—I see it—through wire-
webbed thick glass windows on the mainline—dense with
dark—green growth—flowers, vegetables, small *bonsai*—dark
green—shadows—greenhouse glass ceiling—the prisoner
gardener—beyond bulletproof glass—old-time deep-sea
diver—combs earth blood black—glass globe 1940 World's Fair
logo—enclosed—momentary blizzard set into motion by the
wrist—black as black Bakelite base—trapped—snow petals—
any moment—monkeys—will trapeze into view—day-glo trop-
ical birds—sizzle and squawk—L. Gene in the center of it—
smoking a hand-rolled butt—grinning—aimlessly—he knows
how much is possible—for those—tending a garden—

– * –

Outside—the real garden—overgrown—in the backyard
—
inside—the real book—on—gardening—

– * –

Akiva—knows no—secret—he's from another story—a *koan*—
untied riddle—not-to-wait—sit still—don't—fall down the
well—

Enters—exits—"in peace"—
Buddha—sleep walker—Akiva—brings back—
a dream of four—tana'im—in Pardes—remnants
—as if—we are—awake—

Leave dream—awake—unveil—turn away the pages—slept
within—arise—enter rooms—agreed to be "real"—

—I had a bad dream—impossible to tell it—gets lost in
telling—it sounds—stupid—it makes no sense—another dial-
ing dream: trying to call home—can't see the numbers—
letters—mis-dial—people line-up outside the booth—43 years
of phone dreams—dial—then—touch-tone—

All-seeing Akiva—sees nothing—dialtone—hums wisdom—
full—vacant—absent—present—beyond—within—flow easy—
mystic synonyms—paint gold leaf—auras—halos—around a
sitting saint—unmoving—alive—awake—neither here—nor
there—

The devotees—read—each—silence—enter it—
into a book—they say to each other:—he is—"at once—
at one—with everything"—

– * –

Those who are left are left to figure it out—or—find a
way in—the details remain untold—

What form contained the garden?

Square as the page it grows upon—or a circle—unborn zero from Akiva's alphabet?

Four tana'im enter a square—a circle—(disregard triangle—too pharaonic)—locust squadrons—swords—spear sun-veined mirrors—each feather—petal—erupts upon her gold barge—floats—deathward—upon our blood—overwritten—night calligraphies—

Fill in or empty out or tell—
circle—or square—
cut back—edit—work within borders—
enter the garden—

Say it's *p'shat*—literal—a book—open to a page—we read side by side—on a long bench—sit—before the Book of Paradise—*Sefer ha-Pardes*—literal—as alphabet—four read together—differently—the same words—different keys—*cheder* din—everyone reads aloud—monotonously—melodically—precisely—vaguely—whisper—stammer—shout—sound—text as you can—a texture of voices—rise up—ceiling—roof—vibrate—clusters of *davening* pigeons—doves—*chazonim*—word weavers—en-sounded—noted in each *aut*—

except—Akiva—silent—an unread page

— * —

Shin—shines above the garden—*Aleph*—inspires bees—well of *Mem*—irrigates—even Akiva—

four sun-crowned *kippahs*—seek green shade—pass around—a gourd of drawn water—cold—buried dark—somewhere—a flower—perfume—beyond reason—simmer—sun—tongue probe—blood-orange—ganglia—feasting hummingbirds—

To be here is to disturb it. To be here is wanting to describe it. To tell others something.

Perfume—beyond reason—gold waves—blood—nourishing—
rapturous hummingbirds—ready—to vanish—halos—
outlines—each—rootless—light-devourer—to tell others
something—

light—plays—feathers—spectrum—light—through—hands
and fingers—over their eyes—against *Shin's* glare—
newborn—pink—lumination—light—stored behind each
eyelid—pink light of her sex—his sex—

To be here is to be here with her. To want nothing more. To
be here is to be here with her. To want nothing more.

— * —

Four commentaries—border each telling—on each page—
each—set in their own typeface—

Young saps sawed down in random rows whose wet gummy
bark is pulped into paper.

Four tana'im marked this page with words we turn into com-
mentary bordering a tale.

Not knowing—who wrote the report—four stay fixed—in
writing—objects we subject to names—

— * —

The pure word—erases itself—remains—in the page—the
book—remains—unfinished—page after page—word into
word—you can't recall—it's hard to remember—what's left—

ghosts—traces—one faces—or replaces with enough—
space—around—between—each pure word—woven in white
light—seeking light—to read—black marks—sparks—
wedges—carved into crushed—bleached—membrane-skin—
trees—the marrow memory watches—

reading from reeds—pulped into rolls—unscrolled—rollers and discs—of blackness—each page—memory—memorial—tribute—ancient—present—night sky—page—crowded—alphabet lights—real as words—real signs—not real—hold back its essential—form it other—claim shape—boundary—inside page or name—small claim of witness—and remove—

— * —

It is said: four men, *tana'im*, enter PaRDes; three return.

PaRDeS, the Garden, Paradise, in either sense, inward as instructed, or alive before one's eyes.

Real or dream garden, Paradise or noun. Four men dreaming as one; real as four.

5.

Others

◆

cops everywhere
not stars, imperfect
in shades and uniforms
leather boots
creaking ancient boats
big-beam flashlight
scouring floorboards
seeking seeds and stems

Los Angeles/1957

IT'S SIMPLE

It's simple.
One morning
wake up ready for new work.
Pet the dog.
Dog's not there.
Rise and shine
Sun's not there.

It's simple.
Wake up one morning
ready for new work
and the animals are on strike
with the air, the sea
the earth quits us,
casts us off like a sickness
in her fiery core

(1969)

NIGHT REELS

night when it's light tracked-down on paper
dear haunting light
mere marks mere words sing against dark
tongue furled scoops of milk
O endless possible sea

night canopy our poem shapes
bent over song
long veils down monumental Cocteau hallways
stalled on the Freeway
stammer Ultimate Truth
bent-over peons poem deep
in royal soil, invented earth

night fights like no other
Gillette Blue Blades
left hook tongue knot
hits the deck, out
Lamotta's blond wife in a white suit
speckled with blood
Sugar Ray slams out of Jake's face

night closet to cry in
fur and cloth shields
pain planted deep in dark pockets

dawn scythe alive with song
drive starlight over paper
arise cold bones

skin darkens into night
day after day
the mirror

(1973)

136

KABBALISTIC TREE POEM FOR R. SKRATZ

Silence meets type night collapse of light.

Tree of 10 steps within you
climb up into one moment
then return to real-time.

Or tree of 10 tones
sum total speech
we sing our lives away.

Or tree of 10 lines
less visible
the closer you get.

Or tree of 10 fingers
at birth's hem
touch the newborn crown.
Sun or son
it's bright enough to blind.

Or tree of 10 seeds
sewn into 4 rows of clay.

Or tree of 10 vowels
stolen from the garden
rushed into print
a gold disc millions die for.

Or tree of 10 songs
each more precise than the last
erasing all future all past.

FOR IBN 'ARABI

My problem:
how to think or type kabbalah
while men walk heavy on the roof
installing rain gutters
and young kids cluster below
shrilly singing

how do you turn down the volume?

13 IV 90

I see Asa as I saw him
Iberian frog-prince elegant as Dunhill
brittle clipped British accent
not quite perfect yet no longer Bronx
nor languor of Sephardic Salonika.
Immovable Book we arouse out of
into type's chill against cheek
marking tree skin with song wears death
as life mask whose inner blood silk cape
masks others in an arc of eyebrows and smoke

~ * ~

Phantom Asa inside life's heat
the women arise and ride the mourning ascent
moaning and screaming ululating across transcontinental
        cables
lives bound within plastic receivers
still unable to imagine death

~ * ~

London, 1972

"Ghost is memory
a place I go that's gone
heavy as a book
whose pages age me
my head bowed down with days
as body bends to die
curled-up like a newborn

"I go to a place that's gone
except in snapshots
round brass door-handle
palm-polished

139

"Floorboards footsteps
placing face against window glass
around light's corner

"Death behind and death ahead
memory threads apart
here then gone
everywhere
a ghost"

— * —

Norfolk, 1972

"reet pleat time machine
overflowing pegged cuffs
salted hearts awash within
British Museum scrolls

"Camden town tube station
Camden New Jersey Walt's place
Camden Records' Reb Rosenblatt
singing through time's sandstorms
Camden Town near Nottenham Town
crazy banjos freeze old tunes
as we with mystic coins and sticks and paper
sit at the table and elsewhere
Tony writes you've left London
to green Blue Tile Farm in Stibbard

"Meltzer 5 at Cheval de Trojan
watching the Duke on telly with Don
the dancer of cups and each glass
an ocean and each ocean more information
everything needs translating
books   books   books"

140

— * —

all of it: love, concern, tender irascible purity, formality,
joy of disorder, gone as the eyes of handwriting wobbles
the ardor the hope the love beyond
exilic nostalgia of heart *flaneurs* on a walking-tour of all
the world's ghettos
empty whitewashed *shuls*, cobblestone steps
crooked streets and bolted doors

— * —

what's left behind: your Raziel beside Yetzirah
printer's magic text of primal alphabet
the universe written in a book

— * —

nicotine sonorous voice
—Lit-tle Jack Horner
sat in a corner
eating his Christ-mas pie

—*?Por que lloras, blanca nina?*
?Por que lloras, blanca flor?

You and Pip on Oakie Hill
Tina and I, the four of us in California
listen to Joaquin Diaz

—*Llora por vos, caballero,*
Que vos vas y me dexas.

"Of course I remember this"
and sing along in Ladino
dark resonant filament
eyes closed

—Tengo ninos chiquiticos,
Lloran y demandan pan.
?Si demandan a su padre
Que respuesta les voy a dar?

Abruptly, the next disc
Bud Powell, elegant seismic fury
equally reassuring

◆

maker of riddles and little else
awful power see-saw
impossible bodies
riddled with little else
to declare

want the bent boned poet body
to poke out of the page
my cat-pee sweat stink
real, at least, as the telephone

◆

heart portioned finally shredded to a fine dust in the air
mixing with other less obvious pollutants and irritants

heart no longer synonymous with soul slowly evaporates
        on your
tongue tip

heart on streets in paper cups or caps in thick palimpset of
dirt turned skin into beef-jerky licorice

heart on sleeve insignia of unweaving time

heart in flowers spread ravishing corpses on thick white
        linen
tablecloths customers wait hours to eat on

heart against heart refusing comfort or aid refusing eye
        contact

heart cuffed behind backs in rows on metal benches

heart gone with Cartesian dualism jettisoned into VCR
        Cuisinart
part of the problem solves nothing unifies everything

heart out to lunch with power broker hard-ons with scripts

hearts dark within iconic books

heart attacks its owners anarchy freedom loss

hearts stacked like platters carousel CD hearts in digital
        time
tunnels of irretrievable blessing

hearts in mouths sing yet another song

hearts on parade down Avenue J

♦

how to break the slug in two
its leaky heart bleeds slime
entwined with rapture poets gobble
up trench Romantic mustard-gas dogface
Armory Show then sink into Freud's pomp sofa
talk to be understood her thighs his calves
muscle thrum turn mouth to silk shaft purse
swim out Schreber's unpuckered anus sunrise
dreams reveries broken retold gone
turns against music via cylinder seashell electric
plug in veil wall to wall opera what did it mean
when does it cohere is there anything
cigar-smoke loops the moors
how to wake up how to say it
how to too and why

"STAMPED ON/STRAVINSKY'S/BIRTHDAY"

Hello Martha King
this is "Dave" Meltzer
in the process of writing a poem while it rains
outside and a mockingbird gobbles rotted apples
staked to the backyard fence

Years of GPWITD communiques
young and old voices familiar names and unknowns
all able to write short sweet personal cryptic
a network of others outside with inside gnosis
variably footed

Basil's NYC pencil sketch hangs nearby
a Hebrew alphabet chart and what's to say
between the lines or spaces time unrolls
familiars in paper silence

Hello Martha this David typing light in a room stacked with
books and shelves in piles in disarray all over the place
it's raining the mockingbird wipes its sugar crusted beak
        against
weathered fence slats it's Friday not a rabbi in sight
no minyan nothing but books and papers photos and
        drawings
writing implements everywhere letters tools marking pens
imagining pencils
hello Martha and thanks for and keeps those poems
        coming

(17 vi 91)

146

◆

wood heart sound-board Bach Suite
No. 1 in G Major bowed from a rare cello
bow-hairs over strings hiss in earphones
Yo-Yo Ma where before it was Casals on 78s

wood heart of old Pinocchio
a cricket ready for death O
wooden exits my father bowing his cello
in an empty livingroom

all that's left is wood floor beams
behind sheet-rock walls
doors, stairs, bow's undertow
vibrates soles of feet

heart's wood, wood's wound
music left behind for termites

(2 xi 85)

PRE-

How to open the sky between each word
soon shut, imagined
no matter what or why
it starts you coding

— * —

My table, tablet, pen
ink-well, brown blood
past, the rest.
Who's there?

— * —

My tablet, table, pen
brown ink (blood past)
the poem: who?

— * —

Table, tablet, law in ink
in pen, the poem
(blood past) passes out
of control to its own measure
on blue lines, links of form
from clusters memory serves.

— * —

My what? Mine, my
table, stapled tablet, pen
brown ink, old blood
pulse marks each letter
through time, my rhyme
my what, whose?

148

My table, tablet, pen
brown ink, past blood, over blue lines
following letters into poems.
Who writes?
I transcribe.

~ * ~

Who writes transcribes
not my poem, whose?
11½ p. Brown of the Mound
Bank Street Edinburgh
tablet, Schaeffer's Skrip
brown ink-cartridge in
a Schaeffer pen. No
white or black fire writes each word
into stone, my table belongs to
Alta Bates Hospital.

(17 xii 85)

◆

old love pain chaos the same not the same
son of a man you somewhat resemble
appears like a ghost vanishes unfinished
gnosis left uncircled

new growth new death
woven through earth he disappears within
appears again in a chair
begins typing

◆

Who bends the broken branch back into place
destroys the tree

enough pruning shaping revision
what's rooted reaches deep
is organized to ascend
is mirrored in its own unfolding

the eyes get lost in partiality
the mind invents wholeness in flight from it

(17 i 91)

◆

poem's progress out the door
into another room crowded with rush-hour
smoke pouring out nostrils
a dry-ice effect over brittle pages
natch, no windows
rude pew-like benches
sit on heavy boots profound thoughts
thoroughly modern malaise thickens
hump-beat pulse of chimed words
clot minds alight to drift
a pack of broken oleanders bleed
muse mascara around her eyes
a mask a persona a buried somebody within
mulched inside the unit uprising
in dreams of abounding flesh
the heat's to love the blind embrace
deep turns of memory
nerve ends root after words
write down all en-glyphed
dug into stone, spray-
painted on metal "I
often wonder if she completed
everything she wanted to do
in her life?" note-
taking gathered silence break
pre-school paper chains binding
narrative, image, song

poem's progress pilgrim
bumping nose-to-nose streets
down-looking in arising
grey slabs of dead horizon stored
in stacks of hives shed
thick dust skins stand
stored heaviness mutating

dark oblong blinking book mass
folded-up winged tents
adieux

◆

no more war
in the dark park
lit cigarettes of conspiracy
the men in shadow camouflage
take turns for a crust
between them

no more war for a crust of metal
or grain or scroll
gone before eyes whose light grow night
in cathode bondage
a crust between them
a history, the meaning of groups

no more wars for a crust of touch
walking through holograph divines
porcupined with weapons askew
crunched by democratic Marios
plugged to continuum unplugging their brains
a crust of light a laser-like point
burns a spot on the map
microsurgical scouts scour brain ridges
a dot of memory debriefed

a crust shines like radium in the dark park of bunkers people
sit inside without radios or TV but the smell of waiting and
shadows of phantom light passed around turns their faces into
death masks of unretrievable faith

— * —

how human the loss the found article of clothing she remem-
bers washing now part of a death flag the others gather up
and spread out upon dead ground to sew back into a flag
they'll live beneath and patch together until the country is
completely covered by it driving the lights crazy looking for
a target

153

♦

who's the jew where is he she it that looms up in your face unavoidable hiding behind the scenery manipulating agitating convulsively difficult and wordy

who's the jew on the tree bleached into Aryan calendar art

who's the jew in tubs of intestines and folds of eroticism overwhelming orifices with Wilhold sperm percolating metastasizing permutations of monstrosity

who's the jew in blood of shrugs and connivance pulling back the silken shroud sequentially breaking wings without regard for sound or pain

who's the jew on the freeway wheeling dealing and anxious to please to acquire taboo eliminating all competition

who's the jew inventing America

who's the jew with perfect anonymous plastic generic mask nose thinned lips blue contacts

who's the jew taking inventory of Taiwanese schlock

who's the jew on the tube with his dick in his mouth on overdrive plugging product

who's the jew who knew the waiter at the place everyone pretends not to be jews pretending not to be

who's the jew crossing the line of pubic hairs in mountain-range formation elephantine tongue roots and scavenges for more

who's the jew on stage in putty nose kvetching about who's the jew

who's the jew in church behind a pew smelling of putrid knees who's the jew kids throw ka ka swastikas at tearing away the awning of a gauze temple

who's the jew he she it of corpses and grossness mulching gardens molting meanings constantly overturned

who's the jew wormed inside brains expanding to devour words holding the world together in a perfect circle

who's the jew shrewd ferret weasel alien darkness fouling paper with copyright and power

who's the jew who knew you once when there were no jews

who's the jew you told secrets to

who's the jew we feed to history

who's the jew night gives ink to

who's the jew in chalk-white pies skidding into laughing death

who's the jew who can't say no but won't say yes

who's the jew talking to

who's the jew's friend

who's the jew to you

who are you are you the jew

◆

the poetry that starts
that stops that starts again
the fractal stuff the broken
poetry of a piece a thread
looped through the carpet
binding two cloth zones
into a pants leg marked by red
dashes up and down merged weave

the poetry one steps into
a jacket of sound humming skin
sum of all sounds further fractured
by the speaker's heart
pumping black ink spew
all over their faces

poetry of doors either hinged
or held and moved by pneumatic pipes
heavenly sonorous preposterous
comings and goings

poem of glass slabs slashing air
into slivers of utopia

word of one syllable closing the book

open enigma

(23 iv 91)

♦

old reds to this kid in the ace of knowing
old reds in blue prole denim workshirts
old reds following Robert's rules
old reds with thinning hair consuming huge bosoms
old reds met Friday nights in the storefront
old reds in a row on metal folding chairs
old reds listen intently to ancient seer red
old red sage who'd been there and back and saw the
          impossible
old reds talking walking utopia with oldest red
Comrade Lenin in Brooklyn on a fund-raiser

old reds in gold lit memory reverie
old red fists clenched arms upraised
old reds arise against imbalancing power
old reds resist soul-gobbling machinery
old red hands coiled around sledgehammers
old reds skinny sinewy bony in rolled-up shirtsleeves
old red families picnic on worn park grass May Day fest
old red recalls Big Bill Haywood in Greenwich Village
old reds in a carnival tent hear
Paul Robeson back from the Soviet Union
his silk black basso pops out speaker cones

old reds discuss endlessly Talmudic
old reds want Harlem back and the Depression
old reds want unions back
old reds want to know what to do next
verify demonstrate form a study group exalt
oldest red with piles in British Museum
rubbing frenzies with Rimbaud in the Reading Room
while outside Industry's soot ghosted roar
bombards promethean cathedrals day and night
gigantic blood-inked paper rolls
squash books into stacks tongued through gears
of night terrors seeding momentous activity
whose machines won't stop despite bodies stacking up
pulped by wheels remembered by ancients

in bookstores closing down
Party offices now boiler-rooms run by phone wizards
pulling the plug out of the Good Life
for all you material rubes asleep at the spiel

COMMUTE

the body in the doorway on the sidewalk near the edge
the body poetry's autonomy fails
the stinking body reaching out glazed black
flour-white ankles charcoal toes
piss patina fouled clothing
fist in hot armpit
Night Train blackout frozen sprawl

body on official marble slab
body upright chin down against Burger King wall
body on cement path looking up into sun
cigarette burns brown knuckles

cowled in Baggie rags
shrined on Exit steps
homed behind metal shopping cart
stuffed with bundles
away from poetry's autonomy

I will go home into pages billboards
away from sleeping bodies near the edge
lying dead on the ledge
shuttle up and down BART escalators
commuters locked behind shades
living ghosts refuse damage
go where ghost is cathode
weaving through lost body heat
life rot mulching garments
fused into stale cracked hide

ghosts up and down escalators
sleeping platforms to the sun and moon
wraparound shades high heels tight jaw
lightweight earphones blast digital comfort
office-workers en route out

they go past bodies sliding away
they escape

(1990)

◆

Now sweet when it should be sour
grapes, breaking bones, wisdom asleep
yet one eye open is better than nothing
and nothing's something imagined
another light to read or write by

(4 ix 85)

◆

Alone as the street denies touch
what's there to see, fallen
raw faces swollen enfolded
styptic glint of begging

peeled-back socks
dirt-charred skin
flayed garments
alone as the street disengages
breaks its parts apart
that all may recede
encowled in doorways
passers-by deny

shrines

(19 ii 88)

◆

the pain in paper the pain paper brings
the letters unanswered the unanswered letters
each inked name each death unanswered pain

words meaning then unmeaning then not even blank
      erased
page promising more mort more unanswered letters

— * —

Owl dissembled flaming letters white on black raiments
   of angels feathering brain's veiled ivory
alone aloft but integral and unfolding alphabet of light

(3 ii 88: Robert Duncan [7:00 am])

6.

From *The Art/The Veil* (1981)

The Veil

◆

so sheer between what's right
and will be wronged, let's say
the Taiwanese couple on stage tonight
in their launderette
washing and drying clothing
watched by two teenagers
in a non-descript Duster
windows fogged over with
potsmoke, fear and talk
with one gun between them
and an idea to rob
not for money
but to knife that veil
between them
and the good life

◆

In the hole he counted heartbeats
but got scared they'd stop
listened to broken pipes
under the shit-hole in the floor
finally read the Bible they gave you
but his religion wasn't in a book
unless it's the telephone book
so he stayed alive counting
letters, commas, periods

◆

The veil

existed before he was born
and between his arising
shadowed the world he moved through
reaching for dim forms he thought
brought light

◆

It was perfect
and we're all good at our jobs
but someone imperfect
bumped into the gun
looking somewhere else
and all hell broke loose
but it was only because
we're good at our jobs that
everyone got away clean

◆

The veil

between what's called heart
and the real evil
TV cameras and goons
monitor constant rebellion
whispers, life-
sustaining schemes

Everyone listens for their turn
like Shararazad
keep the axe away another day

◆

The scar

of that moment
without time
clocked rage knife
thrown at Lilith
lands half into my left
pinkie, half onto the table
time begins in sudden pain
wound's mouth pours
reassuring blood onto wood

◆

The veil

the moment nothing is left
no control
a blank
time gone
her kitchen knife in your hand
in her heart
and a new life begins
in old fear running out the door
buried with blood
everything too clear
the lights
no where to go

◆

How cold

outside and inside this iron
I nightly write against
on paper she once wore as bride
down burning stairs
for my love

◆

The piercing

Sunday late noon
a needle through his thumb
straight through it
thread almost laughing
moving in and around
what would no longer be
a fingerprint on file
sworls of skinweb pierced
torn open just a bit
and blood managed out like sap
he sucked
knowing full well there was no snake
except in his head
asleep, mutating

The Art

◆

Organizing these myths these trends these
    traditions these rituals
    this history this pattern
    this secret this hope

Organizing these stars into one bright dot of hot white
        light

As simple as that

◆

Once
each piece of paper
on the desk, the dresser
even on the floor
could be accounted for
there for a reason

♦

It's easier to say nothing
but recently I elaborated.
Yes, I told the reporter
My poems are often connected to on
theme or symbol, long, aspected.
Yesterday all I wrote were haiku,
short and final. No difference.

She took it all down
in shorthand.

♦

Cigarette smoke in my hair
This is the cafe.
I open my mouth
Smoke curls out.
No ghost.
A poet in the bottom
Looking up.

I'm sure it's the city.
I'm a plant not a factory.
Return me to green.
I'll be okay
Watching flowers grow.
Let it rain.
The sky reads me like a book.

♦

Noisily yank a failed poem out of the typewriter roller.
My hair falls into the keys.
Not grey but silver
whose light reminds me of all the work to be done.

♦

It isn't fame or failure
just so many books to read
so many words to write
and the backyard garden's
Paradise.
I could spend all day naming things and
all night breaking promises

◆

Dawn loon silhouette
skims over the lagoon

it's crazed song
unable to tame my rage
into a haiku.

◆

The deception of a new typewriter ribbon
gets him going another few years.

◆

The hunt

in the rain was a failure
her knees in mud
his head hurt from last night
literature left their guns
easy to let go of
rain and more rain
and enough pain to keep them both
alive in themselves as cameos
invoking curses like bullets
like rain like words against nature
ruining their hunt

◆

There's a Europe he holds
inside imagination unfolds
a scrapbook he keeps looking for
his picture among all those beards
dark drowning eyes
keeps looking for a picture of himself
or at least his name on a document
or even a tombstone.
Abruptly Europe dies.
Bloody *tallis* I wave
To cars to eyes. Dies.
The silk blazing.

◆

All the light

he filled blank pages with black ink
repeating primary news
amniotically surrounding vision
before it broke apart
and shadows loom over the survivor
making noises with their mouths

◆

Some enter and never leave
Others go crazy beyond paper
Some know certainty in calligraphy
Nobody can read
And those in between
Scream as pressed flowers

What's given up
given out into her
page whose bones
fan apart.

Peck, carve
attack
bleached membrane.

The edges

where he thought life extended
withdraws into fire-shrinking paper
and all these years his love was paper
his body in a vision resembled a tree

where life retreats a lasso knot
pulled into itself and paper feels like flesh
he's embarrassed watching it withdraw from touch

I go through my body and out onto paper
She wraps my head in white
My eyes burn to read
I can't forget anything
No word or face or silence
They go through my body
Into its streams released
From openings into air
Upon the page

How the world is gone
every moment we are awake in it.

NOTE

The poems in *The Art / The Veil* deal with paradoxes of confinement. Poems in *The Veil* insisted themselves during the years I taught a writing workshop in a State prison. Inmates used the words "outside" and "inside" in a sense I realized were interchangeable and similar to notions a poet might use to describe his/her process of work. *The Art* is about that work. How the inside works its way out and how the outside works its way in.

7.

Notes

K-K-K-A-O-S: LECTURE NOTES
(BIODEGRADABLE PROSE SPECKS)

chaos

k
the letter cutting
a the letter starting
o the alarm
s the snake again

How it began isn't at issue nor is it what's brought forth.
How it went is where we are at the edges pulling in lines
to weave baskets grids stick out of.
How it goes is where we rush the border to break the wall
     down
the platforms of the book the pages enraged it unravels
     its sprung
reels attacking the eye already deluged by sign.
How it will be as it is in hell and heaven imagined and
     invented
scouring the light for dark armament.
How it could be breaks the circuit-board.

Why did it happen the goddess taped to the ceiling began
     moving?
Why did they open the backdoor to afternoon reclaiming
     everyday?
Why did the duds of alchemy sequin the curse of their
     limit?
Why did the closed system wheel out of screen and halve
     the
holistic magus in gown splattered abstract expressionism
     blood?

The chaos in the field whose form is dogma.
The chaos is figure face and goblet in hand-out chapbook
     of optical allusions.
The metaphor in transit wed to weeds of chaos alarming
     the
perfect mower of code-lines

The meta- and master-phor of phosphorus powders
        alarmed in flash
the static posture bound to death.
Where was it first found embedded in dead weave of tree
        skin.
Ink radiant spectrum in each carved valley of word.

— * —

preformed chaos
strives to form
into play and ploy
plot and lore of discourse
        (dominant or
        otherwise, or are there
        other ways of) insisting
order comes through language

Then, on course, the poem before its glyphic styptic
        incisions

Chaos is invariably afterward, after word has nourished it
into semblance, priority
its prior otherness was face-less or form-less
its past was undescribed until emerging into light of page

No need for "it" to be ineffable when the stuff before us
in auras of shrink-wrap begs to transcend

Chaos is process the fixed frozen specter breaks into
for its own glory

Before we know it, it is; continuing after we've named it

Heraclitus: *The saying is their witness: absent while
        present.*

formal assumptions, assumptions of form: they form
utopian landscapes writing maps

who looks into the core of what was chaos looks for form
what looks back has to be shaped into something
        manageable
the imagination limits itself in its need to shape

Big utterances across white space.

Measure the form breath impresses on paper as air.
What's noted as fixed and/or rigid becomes solved and
        resolved;
it is said to be formal and/or structural. We delight in
dismantling what has become clear enough to identify in
        all its
workings.

                        — * —

Indo-European root: *ghi*: open wide. Greek, *chasm. chaos.*
Jan Baptista von Helmont (d. 1644), who is credited for coin-
ing the word *gas,* said he based it on the word *chaos*; but
Paracelsus (d. 1541) used the word *gas* to mean air.

Indo-European root: *cal*: good-looking, beautiful.
Greek *kallos*: beauty. *kaleidophone*: instrument to make
sound waves visible in patterns of light. *kaleidoscope.*
calligraphy.

empty space
often seen as space
filled beyond seeing
what's there, i.e.,
death-camp bodies in piles
stacked on flatbed trucks
pulling away from the camera

                        — * —

memory as chaos; chaos as memory

"When we learn something there must be a change in the
brain, but no one knows what the change is.

"The code of the nervous system is provided basically by the
fact that each nerve fiber carries only one sort of information.
Memory thus depends upon selection from the original mul-
tiplicity of possible actions of those that represent the useful
response to the environment."

[From: *The Oxford Companion to the Mind*; edited by Richard L. Gregory, 1987.)

How to imagine what's inside the mind other than chaos. What's a "well-ordered" mind look like, work like? Is it another invention to girdle chaos, or are we talking about a process, a dialectical continuum, something quintessential, symbiotic?

Chaos describes itself in the ordered vanishing of language.

Chaos invites (tempted to write "demands") creation. Creation resists chaos, insists on order, hidden or revealed. Creation contain; chaos is boundless.

Magnifiable differences between one culture's sense of order and another's perception of dis-order. Abounding difference.

"Can't see the trees for the forest."

On the shelf: *Man's Rage for Chaos: Biology, Behavior and the Arts* by Morse Peckham (1965).

Compulsive, phobic, panic for form, for order.

Margins everywhere; put there by disequiliberated citizens.

"Chaos" associated w/ "wildness" wilderness and the Romantic retreat to nature behind modernity's smokestacks

notes

letters, markings, spread out on the page in a language unfamiliar to the reader: another aspect of chaos

imagining death, the moment, or birth

Aleph: One

In the beginning. He/She/It/That. What is separate yearns for chaos, initial state of being, without language, being undifferentiated, unconditioned stuff, unconditional, the unific dynamic of chaos one comes shaped out of, separated from

in the pressure of answer, the splinter of glass sees only eye
blood, the I and the eyes "having it" unless dyslexic or aphasic
where the word and world's restored to selfless flow its
speakers might name "chaos"

rubbing wrong ways
rubbing-out last strand of words and de-railing syntax
bursting out of bordered sentence mazes
breaking-out of the joint seeking freedom

lethal sequence duration, the noise of discharge enveloping
the murderer in chaos of rage and passion

possession—*dybbuk* or *loa* emptying-out the mind—erasing
self layers—

to re-member put together pieces from the Nile of memory

to forget is chaos
we repeat the beads to order and focus
remember transitory allure of being

chaos of blank page

chain-link fence pit-bulls hurl muscled flanks against
barking at your eyes

sneeze orgasm laughter
we exit through chaos

poem sutured into shaved skin at cranial North Pole

before beginning, ending

New College of California, 1990

MILLENNIAL

it expects to be announced

no one has a clue except those flapping floppy Bibles in
        your
face

even anticipating *something* is a tip-off

forget it
the vocabulary of travel
of getting somewhere
going someplace
arriving

it's gone before the hangover kicks in

whatever happens is theatrical, i.e., in obeyance to the
        sacred
script

who's coming for anything? even dinner?
the Messiah? Utopia?
trance-ending transcendence?
who's there? what's up?

inside a Tupperware globe cowl with punched-out eye-holes
whatever I see is what I'm looking for

doubt's the fuel that burns the bed with hope

an American flatness, an image, extreme cartoon void of
        midrange,
a hologram paper doll desires credit, dresses and redresses

look forward to what?
more of the same, the sameness of more

look forward to what?
violent wealth, mutilating poverty

look forward to what?
progress returns to nowhere
where we find our stores empty or gorged with goods

looking forward looks backward

looking forward looks back to words promising a future
here and horrid

looking forward for words to work as bullet-proof vests

looking for words to eat

or really not looking anywhere
not even within
let creepy kids sleep

really not looking but seeing everything look away

looking away the way subtle or obvious villains on TV do

looking away the way one walks away from an open hand

looking away the way power pimps declare innocence
turning away to whisper to attorneys

looking away while evil disperses into the commonplace

in a rut of glut

a tub of electric fish
a glue of rust
in a glance a bullet breaks our spell
in a rush to future's past
in a hurry to score to intake partake
a moment out of time out of money
in a rut stunned by loss

nobody looks down on their way to pay
for play that won't stay in place
replacing everything with everything else
until nothing looks good
nothing looks back
nothing looks straight ahead
doesn't wince in blaze of lights
plugged into mini-cams circling prey
helicopters roto-tilling night
nothing talking millennium
nothing doing
nothing done

no one's got a hint but something's wanted
don't lock the door
keep walking away from the sound
pay monthly dues
sing shoeless blues
watch unused body darken
watch unused muscles soften with sot
watch unused kids fill air with death
watch unused outcasts blast glass apart
watch unused animals pace back and forth
watch and wait and sleep through all particulars
insomniac defender against all noise alien to dialtone

diversely uniform
class-coded tiered torment choirs
orgasmic cables lasso body politic
laocoon replay tears hearts out of beginners
cancel as many lives as possible
planet's going down the toilet
refuse hands eyes of the fallen
club all clans claiming community
dance in broken mirror workshops
tommygun therapeutic aerobic pillow-eaters
drown diving for pearl of self

what sign O seer
sun and moon laser stippled Happy Face eclipse

192

fussing over civility routines
suffering machines of debility
keep up appearing
step up with protocol
interact on oilspill
slip into interface
network coded digitalized hiss
locust tapping keyboard PC enthralled
what sign O seer what omen between the lines

it expects itself
it is already being denounced
no one has a clue despite piling floppies
anticipating rips out another row of sutures
doubt fuels hope
flat future re-runs
sameness of more

(1994)

Printed July 1994 in Santa Barbara & Ann
Arbor for the Black Sparrow Press by Mackintosh
Typography & Edwards Brothers Inc. Text set in
Benguiat by Words Worth. Design by Barbara Martin.
This edition is published in paper wrappers;
there are 200 hardcover trade copies;
100 copies have been numbered & signed
by the author; & 26 lettered copies have been
handbound in boards by Earle Gray each with
an original drawing by David Meltzer.

Photo: Tina Meltzer

DAVID MELTZER is the author of several books of poetry including *Tens*, edited by Kenneth Rexroth (McGraw-Hill), *Yesod* (Trigram Press), *Six* (Black Sparrow Press), *Bark: A Polemic* (Capra Press), *Harps* (Oyez), *The Name* (Black Sparrow Press), and *Arrows: Selected Poetry, 1957-1992*. He has edited various thematic anthologies including *The San Francisco Poets: Interviews* (Ballantine Books), *The Secret Garden: Classical Kabbalistic Texts* (Continuum), *Birth: Texts, Songs, Prayers, and Stories* (North Point Press) and the recently published *Reading Jazz* (Mercury House). *Orf*, one of ten erotic novels he wrote in the 60s, has been recently reprinted by Rhinoceros Books; The Agency trilogy, first published in the 60s, will be reprinted by Richard Kasak/Masquerade Books. Vanguard Records has reissued his 60s rock band's first album *Serpent Power*, on CD. Current projects include an anthology of culture war texts, *High/Low Browse*, a critical work on popular culture: *Everyday Myth*, and a biographical study of the influential Los Angeles artist Wallace Berman. With poet Clark Coolidge, vocalist/songwriter Tina Meltzer, and assorted musicians, poets, and artists, he is part of MIX, a performance ensemble. Meltzer teaches in both the undergraduate Humanities program and the graduate Poetics program at New College of California in San Francisco.